"*Gospel Mom* pairs refreshing insight with a practical exploration of what it means to let the gospel influence your motherhood in the questions that matter most."

—RUTH CHOU SIMONS,
mom to six, bestselling author, artist, and founder of gracelaced.com

"Emily and Laura have written the book I wish I'd had when my children were younger. *Gospel Mom* is both deeply biblical and extremely practical. It offers real help in knowing how to believe and apply the gospel in the moments of your day. If you want to love Jesus and be more like him as you labor in the high calling of parenting, this is the book for you."

—COURTNEY DOCTOR,
Bible teacher and author of *From Garden to Glory*

"We all know the feeling of trying to apply someone else's solution to our season of motherhood: it often doesn't fit, and it leaves us wondering if there is real and lasting help for the challenges we face. In *Gospel Mom,* readers will behold with fresh eyes the wonder of how the gospel of Jesus really does change *everything*. Each mom will find a home in these pages. See how the gospel can transform every unique season of motherhood for your joy, for the world's good, and for God's glory."

—AMY GANNETT,
author of *Fix Your Eyes* and founder of Tiny Theologians

"If you're wondering what it means to live out your faith in the ups and downs of parenting, look no further than Emily Jensen and Laura Wifler's newest book, *Gospel Mom*. This book delves deeply into what it means to be a mom who knows the truths of the Scriptures and lives them out in the daily routines of family life. *Gospel Mom* is a needed encouragement that will refresh your heart with biblical insight and help you navigate parenting decisions with wisdom and grace."

—MELISSA KRUGER,
author and vice president of discipleship programming at The Gospel Coalition

"We desire to make the best choices for our families but often don't know where to begin. In our desperation, we search the internet for answers to all our tough motherhood questions. In *Gospel Mom*, Emily Jensen and Laura Wifler provide a better solution: the hope of the gospel and a practical framework for the daily challenges of motherhood, pointing moms to the joy, rest, and peace found in God's Word. No matter where you are in your motherhood journey, *Gospel Mom* will encourage you and equip you to live for the glory of God."

—GRETCHEN SAFFLES,
author of *The Well-Watered Woman* and founder of Well-Watered Women

"*Gospel Mom* is the gift I want to give every mama—the power to preach the gospel to herself in every situation. Through the framework of Creation, Fall, Redemption, and Consummation, Emily and Laura equip mothers with the only message we really need. This is a fantastic resource for both new and seasoned mothers who desire to embrace the grace of the gospel and share it with others."

—HUNTER BELESS,
writer, podcaster, and creator of Journeywomen Ministries

"*Gospel Moms* invites us to ditch the elusive pursuit of a formulaic approach to motherhood and embrace a gospel framework that encourages women to think biblically rather than emotionally or experientially. It meets a mom in the grit of the mundane and lifts her eyes to the glorious, majestic joy and freedom found only in the gospel."

—KAREN HODGE,
author and coordinator of women's ministries for the Presbyterian Church in America

"In an era dominated by curated social-media depictions of idealized motherhood, *Gospel Mom* serves as a refreshing antidote. It peels back the layers of guilt, comparison, and identity crisis that so often plague mothers, providing a roadmap to a parenting journey filled with joy and grace."

—MARY A. KASSIAN,
author and mom

GOS PEL MOM

EMILY A. JENSEN & LAURA WIFLER

HARVEST HOUSE PUBLISHERS
EUGENE, OREGON

Unless otherwise indicated, all Scripture verses are taken from the ESV® Bible (The Holy Bible, English Standard Version®), copyright © 2001 by Crossway, a publishing ministry of Good News Publishers. Used by permission. All rights reserved.

Scripture verses marked CSB have been taken from the Christian Standard Bible®, Copyright © 2017 by Holman Bible Publishers. Used by permission. Christian Standard Bible® and CSB® are federally registered trademarks of Holman Bible Publishers.

Verses marked NIV are taken from the Holy Bible, New International Version®, NIV®. Copyright © 1973, 1978, 1984, 2011 by Biblica, Inc.™ Used by permission of Zondervan. All rights reserved worldwide. www.zondervan.com. The "NIV" and "New International Version" are trademarks registered in the United States Patent and Trademark Office by Biblica, Inc.™

Verses marked NASB are taken from the (NASB®) New American Standard Bible®, Copyright © 1960, 1971, 1977, 1995 by The Lockman Foundation. Used by permission. All rights reserved. www.lockman.org.

Verses marked NLT are taken from the Holy Bible, New Living Translation, copyright © 1996, 2004, 2015 by Tyndale House Foundation. Used by permission of Tyndale House Publishers, Inc., Carol Stream, Illinois 60188. All rights reserved.

Published in association with the literary agency of Wolgemuth & Wilson.

Art direction and cover design by Nicole Dougherty
Cover concept by Bryce Williamson
Interior design by Janelle Coury
Artwork © Ninterints / Creative Market

For bulk, special sales, or ministry purchases, please call 1-800-547-8979.
Email: CustomerService@hhpbooks.com

This logo is a federally registered trademark of the Hawkins Children's LLC.
Harvest House Publishers, Inc., is the exclusive licensee of this trademark.

Gospel Mom

Copyright © 2024 by Emily A. Jensen and Laura Wifler
Published by Harvest House Publishers
Eugene, Oregon 97408
www.harvesthousepublishers.com

ISBN 978-0-7369-8852-0 (hardcover)
ISBN 978-0-7369-8853-7 (eBook)

Library of Congress Control Number: 2024930082

Printed in China

24 25 26 27 28 29 30 31 32 / RDS / 10 9 8 7 6 5 4 3 2 1

To our children:

Lewis, Gabe, Cal, Jones, Eveline

and Eli, Colette, Eden

ACKNOWLEDGMENTS

There's a phrase in motherhood, taken from an ancient African proverb, that says, "It takes a village to raise a child." And it's true of writing books too. We've not only been shaped by teachers, theologians, pastors, and mentors over the years, but we've benefited from practical support from our husbands, parents, in-laws, friends, and colleagues. While most people flip past the acknowledgments, we hope you'll pause to read about the village that helped make this book possible—because we couldn't have done it alone.

To our husbands, Brad and Mike, we know you share in this sacrifice most of all and are our closest confidants and supporters. Thank you for continuing to cheer us on and encourage us to prioritize this ministry, which was unexpected for all of us.

To our children, Lewis, Gabe, Cal, Evie, and Jones, and Eli, Colette, and Eden: We know it's hard when Mom has to spend extra time away to write, but we're grateful for your sacrifice and patience. We hope that someday you'll see how you so greatly contributed to the kingdom of God.

To our parents and in-laws, Henry and Gayla Grayum, Dean and Dianne Jensen, and Vicki and Scott Brace: We know that when deadlines get tight or we need to travel, you're the first to raise your hands to sweep in with practical help and prayer. Thanks for always supporting and rejoicing in the work we do.

Andrew Wolgemuth has been the founding big brother of our writing careers, and his faithful leading and investment in our lives over the past years are part of the reason we have our dream jobs. We're grateful for your wise and steady voice and the many opportunities you've helped us obtain and discern. The Harvest House team, especially Kyle Hatfield, were also some of the first to see us as authors and invest in the message and mission of Risen Motherhood and what it might mean to the kingdom. Also to Bob Hawkins, Barb Sherrill, Heather Green, and the whole Harvest House family: We love what you stand for and the work you encourage.

When we realized how much we were trying to tackle in this book, we knew we'd need lots of extra eyes to help us make sure we were communicating with truth and clarity. Thank you to Kelsey Hency for working through our earliest draft of the manuscript and providing excellent feedback. Also, a huge thanks to Jen Wilkin for your sharp eyes and wise feedback. Your support of Risen Motherhood over the years has meant so much to us.

To the Risen Motherhood team: You are truly such a gift to us. It's been such a joy to work alongside like-minded women for the sake of the gospel. Your organization, support, and leadership helped us take the time away that we needed to write this book.

To our church families at Grand Avenue and Cornerstone Church, especially our pastors and small groups: You have prayed for us, shaped us, and cultivated so much of this through your teaching and example. We love you and are grateful for you.

And last, but most importantly—we love you, Lord. We're simply your messengers, and we're not even the best or the brightest you could have sent. Thank you for letting us participate in your work. May you multiply the fruit of the gospel in and through this book.

CONTENTS

Part 3: The Thinking

Conclusion: Gospel Mom

Appendixes

HOW TO GET THE MOST
OUT OF THIS BOOK

When we were developing the concept for this book, we knew that it would include a lot of dense information and opportunities for personal reflection. Like any other skill we learn, there is an element of reading, watching, and listening but also an important step of trying it on your own. That's why, from the very beginning, we created a companion workbook, *Becoming a Gospel Mom*, to accompany this book. While the companion workbook isn't essential to understanding our framework for applying the gospel to motherhood, we do think it is immensely helpful, as you may see some of these concepts mapped out in different ways and have lots of application questions and space to process your own situation. Gospel motherhood is rooted in Christ, but the way it plays out is deeply personal. We hope you'll consider snagging the workbook to help you think through some of these things for yourself or with a group.

INTRODUCTION:
WHAT KIND OF MOMS?

Mothers, it turns out, really do love a formula.

When our ministry, Risen Motherhood, first began to grow and require more time, the golden question was: How does work *work*? We each wondered: Exactly how many hours can I spend on this without compromising my motherhood? We were both moms of young children and primarily spent our days focused on the needs of our homes, but the Lord seemed to have additional plans for our days. We were deep in discussions about the gospel and motherhood, and we wanted to know what it looked like for a believing mom to be faithful while also pursuing other callings. Working at Risen Motherhood meant we needed occasional time away from our children for focused work and travel. We tried to make an equation by stringing together wise inputs of decision-making: *personal circumstances* plus *theological truth* plus *wise counsel* multiplied by *prayer* and divided by *practical implications*. As we thought through this, we each prayed and sought counsel from others who knew us well in real life, all to find the perfect number of hours a mom could work and still be a "good Christian mom."

Spoiler alert: We never did find that number.

But it turned out the Lord didn't need us to follow the right formula to provide wisdom and guidance for our own lives. Over time, he brought both of us to places of peace and freedom in our motherhood, with our husbands, and in our work. He didn't give us the exact number of work hours, days, or trips he'd always intended for moms in Iowa to commit to a calling and still be considered faithful. Instead, he worked in our lives through his Word and his people, leading us in ways that were unique to us as we followed him in faith.

We didn't realize it at the time, but wanting standard, easy-to-understand answers and formulas is a common feeling in nearly every area of motherhood. And not just for us but for moms everywhere. Look at nearly any survey of mothers, and you'll find the majority of them struggle with guilt or feel overwhelmed. For just one example, in our annual Risen Motherhood survey, 93 percent of the nearly 10,000 moms who responded said they experience mom guilt.[1] We're guessing that some of that has to do with the fact that most of us moms aren't sure whether we're *doing* motherhood right. Moms love their kids, and moms want clarity about what it takes to parent with excellence. So we look for places and people who seem to have the instruction manual for parenting.

Imagine this scene with us: Eager parents-to-be sit sprawled on a nursery floor in the midst of parts and pieces, baskets, and empty boxes, hovering over a project as they anticipate the arrival of their first baby. Though arguments arise and assembly starts and stops, they help each other through the step-by-step instructions as they pass a manual back and forth. It all goes slower than expected, but eventually, together they step back to admire their handiwork. The crib looks just like the picture they saw online.

Maybe you didn't live this scene, or maybe it's similar to your own experience. Either way, you probably know the desire to prepare for motherhood and want everything to go just so. But while cribs and changing tables come with instructions, much of the work of raising children does not.

[1] "The Results Are In! Our 2022 Survey of Christian Motherhood," Risen Motherhood, March 24, 2022, https://www.risenmotherhood.com/articles/the-results-are-in-our-2022-survey-of-christian-motherhood.

While recipes, math problems, and new toys benefit from clear, predictable step-by-step instructions, mothering isn't as simple as input-output. In the absence of a handbook or formula that outlines exactly what we need to do the "right" things in parenting—down to the SKU number and sleep-training style—we stare into the abyss of 18-plus years with nothing but the advice of millions to comfort us. Without a clear process and the perfect next step, we're left to cobble together our own picture of what motherhood should look like.

Some people start with their own mother, updated and refreshed with the latest trends. *She did a pretty good job—maybe I can just be like her.* Some women cringe at the thought of becoming like their mother and instead reject her image completely, setting out to be the opposite. If neither of those options seems right, we might construct our picture out of pieces from our mother-in-law, our best friend who just became a mom two years ahead of us, or the young moms from our church. Or perhaps we find a few moms on social media and decide to buy from all their links and subscribe to all their methods. Every effort to figure out what to do as a mom feeds our larger questions: What kind of mom should I be? *And what makes me that kind of mom?*

At the core of these questions is the desire to be a good mom. By God's common grace, most moms are hard-wired with a deep longing to nurture, love, and protect their children—giving them all good things. We want to get it right because we feel the weight of our responsibility for the lives we hold. We love our children, and we comprehend the stakes of getting it wrong. These desires are also laced with other longings—the longing to know that we're enough. That we've done a good job. That our lives matter. We want other people to notice and give us credit for the good that we do and admire us for it. We hope that someday, maybe, as our child accepts some prestigious award, they'll look directly into the camera and say, "I dedicate this to my amazing mom, who made me who I am today. I wouldn't have any of this without her."

But that day isn't today. Snap back to reality, and we are the mother cradling her hand on the small of her back as she smooths the other hand over the life growing inside her. Or the mom with two under two, holding a child on each hip. Or the mom racing to get her three teenagers out the door in the morning. At each stage, we look out the window and wonder, *What does it take to be a good mom?*

Fill-in-the-Blank Mom

Over the last decade, the two of us (Emily and Laura) have embarked on our own journeys to understand what a good mom really is. If you read our first book, *Risen Motherhood: Gospel Hope for Everyday Moments*, then you might know that as sisters-in-law and friends, we talked regularly, discussing our everyday experiences as new moms. While we were asking each other questions about how we thought Scripture guided us in decisions about first foods, naptime routines, and working outside the home, we didn't yet realize that we were asking something even deeper. Eventually, those questions became a whole ministry dedicated to living "Risen Motherhood," and throughout the years, we explored hundreds of daily topics, seeking to apply overarching truths from God's Word to motherhood. Ten years into our own motherhood journeys, something started to crystallize for us—we were the moms who want to know not just *what to do* but *who to be.*

We've seen moms try to answer this question in a myriad of ways. And of course, we've done it ourselves too. It's like we all imagine a blank line before the word *mom*, and then we fill in that blank with anything we can until we find something that feels like a fit. The thought process, though often subconscious and complex, might cycle through subcultures and stereotypes: homesteading mom, urban mom, overseas-missionary mom, crunchy mom, gentle-parenting mom, homeschool mom, empowered mom, trendy mom, influencer mom, stay-at-home mom, career mom, chill mom, clean-living mom, I-do-what-I-want mom, you-can't-put-me-in-a-box mom, and so on.

Deep down, it seems like if we can just find the right word to fill in the blank, it will shore up our wavering hearts and give us the assurance we need that we have measured up on the scoreboard. If we just get the right picture, we have a model. And for many of us, the model means there can be a handbook. And a handbook means we can finally have a formula for motherhood, erasing (or at least easing) the questions, fears, and ambiguities of our role. A tangible model for motherhood means we can be a little more sure that we're doing it "right" and have a measuring stick to check our progress.

But here's the catch—no matter how much we try to model ourselves after a certain type of mom (or maybe we're the mom who just waffles as she tries to find her type at all), we'll never be able to execute it perfectly. We'll find that we fall short and can't keep up in certain areas. Or that life hands us trials, sorrows, and circumstances neither we nor the manual were expecting. We might find that for a time, we can hold it all together according to our cultural model, but that often leads to us becoming smug and judgmental moms who are convinced we've found the one right way of being good while everyone else is falling short. Eventually, all of us find that we're still not totally happy with the mom we are, and we're left longing and questioning.

The good news, is our bent to fill in the space before *mom* is a good one. There is a word that can fill in the blank before *mom* and lead us into faithful parenting. And it's probably not the word you've been searching for.

Gospel Moms

If you've read *Risen Motherhood*, then you've heard us share a bit about God's purpose for moms:

> God's design [for motherhood], both physically and spiritually, reflects the heart of the greatest Life Giver to the world. He is the ultimate creator of life, the ultimate nurturer and provider, and the compassionate gentle one who supplies our needs when— like our own babies—our only capacity is to cry for help…Until Christ returns, mothers have the mission of duplicating life and being fruitful through the Great Commission by the power of

the Holy Spirit. Our mothering should point our husbands, children, churches, and communities toward knowing and loving the same gospel we love.[2]

The purpose of our motherhood is ultimately rooted in God and his good design. It's not about us; it's about him. As women created in God's image, we exist to "glorify God and enjoy him forever."[3] We do that first and foremost by acknowledging the "bad news" that we are sinners who fall short of the glory of God and have no ability to accomplish this purpose by ourselves. Then, by believing and confessing the gospel or "good news" that Jesus Christ came to save sinners through his life, death, and resurrection, we're made new.

This gospel story has undergirded our whole ministry at Risen Motherhood. Knowing Christ changes everything about who we are and how we live. It isn't just about one moment in history where Jesus hung on a Roman cross; it encapsulates a story that we are invited to be a part of, and it gives us the answers to our deepest longings and questions. As the gospel compels us to look to Christ, we learn who we really are, who we need, and who we should be. We start to understand our past and look forward to our future. We discover where we can get life, hope, help, joy, peace, rest, love, comfort, strength, and so much more. We find answers to our questions. Our identities are secured so that no matter what happens to us or how we stumble, we're safely bound to Christ, all the way through, until we reach home.

Much could be said about this—we've already written a whole book about it, and we're going to unpack it more in this one! But for now, here's what we want you to know: God does have a person he wants you to model your life after, and that person is his son, Jesus Christ. God doesn't give you

---

[2] Emily Jensen and Laura Wifler, *Risen Motherhood: Gospel Hope for Everyday Moments* (Eugene: Harvest House Publishers, 2019), 37, 38.

[3] "Shorter Catechism of the Assembly of Divines: The 1647 Westminster Confession and Subordinate Documents," A Puritan's Mind, accessed November 29, 2022, https://www.apuritansmind.com/westminster-standards/shorter-catechism/.

a formula or a precise point-by-point, product-by-product guide for every minute decision in motherhood, but he does give you his Word, with all the instructions you need to know to walk wisely through your motherhood journey. God doesn't leave you to figure all of it out on your own. He gives you his Spirit (and the church) to empower, help, and guide you along the way.

So you want to know what kind of mom to be? A Gospel Mom.[4]

We will explore this concept more throughout the book, but in case you need some convincing right up front, we hope you see that this kind of mom is full of joy and freedom.

A Gospel Mom...

Gains a new heart and a new nature with Christ's righteousness. You do good not to earn anything but because good has been done for you and you know you are capable of following and obeying God's commands.

Knows her mission and purpose. No matter your earthly accolades, you live a life sold out for Christ, displaying his goodness to the world around you and sharing the reason for the hope that you have.

Lives free from the punishment of sin yet still wrestles with its power. You won't be perfect, and you will struggle with this tension of a sin nature until you reach heaven's shores. You know God is in the business of redemption—nothing is too far gone or too bad for him to redeem.

---

[4] When people use the word *gospel*, they can mean different things. For the purpose of this book and how we're framing motherhood, we're using the word *gospel* to represent the metanarrative of God's redemption story through Christ for his people. The story of the good news of Jesus Christ is all-encompassing, and it also impacts all of life. The grand story of redemption is the one that informs all of our other roles and decisions. The mnemonic CFRC (Creation, Fall, Redemption, Consummation) is the tool we use to help ourselves and other moms remember the high-level points of this narrative so we can more quickly consider how they apply. We were not the originators of this idea—it's been commonly used throughout church history in various traditions. We've learned from a wide variety of Christian authors and theologians over the years as we've developed our thinking about how CFRC interplays with our unique circumstances, personal conscience, and heart motivations.

Understands the realities of a broken earth and the hardship of life east of Eden. You know suffering and sorrow will be constant companions throughout your days on earth, and you don't expect life to always be easy.

Lives free from mom guilt. Because there is no condemnation for those who are in Christ and your sins are fully paid for, you don't have to suffer under the suffocating weight of mom guilt. If you're struggling, you can dig under the surface and uncover whether you're experiencing true conviction from the Holy Spirit or condemnation as you fail to meet your own or your culture's ideals.[5]

Rejoices because nothing can separate her from the love of God. When you fail, you can tell God, repent, and keep trusting him. He isn't mad at you or disappointed. He loves you more than you can ever imagine. You know God promises to help you, through the guidance of his Word and his Spirit and other people around you.

Recognizes the battle is against the world, the flesh, and the devil—not other moms. You know the battle isn't really about methods, ideas, or opinions on motherhood but instead against the spiritual forces of evil. You know who the true enemy is, and you stand your ground.

Walks in freedom from fear. While you know there are many things you could fear in this life, ultimately you only fear the Lord and believe that he is in control of all things. You rest secure that it's not up to you to control every variable or protect from all harm.

Trusts God to continue to grow and change her. You know you are sealed with the promise of the Holy Spirit, who is living and active inside of you, growing you day by day into the likeness of Christ.

---

[5] See appendix C for more help unpacking mom guilt.

Sets her sight on eternity and the glory that awaits. You don't live for the immediate rewards of today in your marriage or kids, your bank account, or your circumstances. Your gaze is fixed on the person and work of Christ and what matters for eternity. You live with hope and a future.

Where We're Headed

In this book, we want to help you fill the blanks in your motherhood with the word *gospel* and live the type of motherhood we've laid out above by showing you how to navigate your everyday decisions and current circumstances with joy and freedom as you follow Christ. We believe this happens through a comprehensive understanding of the gospel in God's Word, the regular practice of spiritual disciplines and habits, and knowing how your circumstances, personal conscience, and heart motivations can help or hinder you as you bring glory to God. We want you to learn that a Gospel Mom isn't loyal to a modern lifestyle or method, subculture, or stereotype. She doesn't just blindly copy her mom or her friends at church or her favorite influencer. She's loyal to the King of kings and submits to his leading in all things.

To start this book, we will be giving you an overview and a short look at the life of a Gospel Mom, and then we'll spend the rest of the book explaining what we mean and digging deeper. We've created the companion workbook, *Becoming a Gospel Mom,* so you can follow along, make notes, and work through what gospel motherhood might look like in your own life.

If you are familiar with us and our Risen Motherhood ministry, then you are used to us showing you our approach to motherhood through our own application. That is what we did in the *Risen Motherhood* book and what we've done on hundreds of podcast episodes, but this book is a little different. One of our hopes in writing this book was to truly pull back the curtain and take time to explain our thought process as we approach motherhood in light of the gospel. You might think of this book as a gospel primer for moms or a master class in applying truths of Scripture to motherhood and remembering the pillars and principles we've learned to consider along the way.

We want to make it clear that if you've believed in the good news of Jesus, you don't need any fancy Christian books on motherhood (yes, even this one) to glorify God, because you're fully righteous before the throne of God through Christ and have the Holy Spirit inside you. As a believer, you are already glorifying God as you look to him, live for him, and make decisions in faith. Just like the gospel itself is both beautifully simple and infinitely deep, living as a Gospel Mom is both simple (*just live by the Word of God and follow him in faith!*) and complex (*study, consider, apply wisdom, and spend time in prayer to seek God's leading, will, and praise in every moment of life*). We're sharing the concept of Gospel Moms with you not to give you another thing to have to achieve or worry about but as a helpful aide along the way. But with or without this book or way of thinking, we trust that if you're following Christ, this good news will keep doing its work in your heart and life.

The book is organized in three parts: the framework, the practices, and the thinking.

The Framework

In part 1, we'll walk you through the four parts of the gospel narrative—Creation, Fall, Redemption, and Consummation (CFRC)—helping you grasp the meaning of those terms for yourself and understand why they matter in your daily life and decisions.

The Practices

In part 2, we'll lay out some common and important gospel practices and how they scaffold the life of a Gospel Mom. This includes things like spiritual disciplines, living in Christian community, and practicing regular rhythms of rest.

The Thinking

In part 3, we'll help you think through a lot of gray areas of motherhood as you seek to apply the gospel and follow God's leading in your life. We'll explain personal conscience and help you evaluate your own unique circumstances and motivations. We'll conclude with a look at the overarching goal of a Gospel Mom—to do all things to the glory of God and continue to grow in his likeness, knowing that we won't always get it right but we can rest in what faithfulness and success look like in God's economy no matter what.

We Are Gospel Moms

Let's go back to the scene from earlier in the chapter. The same parents who were once sprawled out on the nursery floor reading a manual to assemble a crib are gazing down at their precious new baby. The mother reaches in and scoops up her baby girl. The new mom is scared and unsure, but as she cradles her daughter gently, she whispers a prayer. You can't see what the mom is thinking behind her slight smile, but if you could read her thoughts, you'd know that she's at rest. God will give her grace for the challenges that lie ahead. God will give her help and guidance. God will be with her, and he loves her daughter more than she ever could.

Eventually, the crib is swapped out for a toddler bed, then a twin bed, then a bunk bed. The parents go in and out of the room over the years, assembling different furniture and redecorating as their daughter grows. Tossings and turnings, tears and toddler tantrums, tough conversations, and teenage woes rush through like movie scenes. When nearly two decades have passed, boxes and baskets again line the walls—she's leaving for college. When every item is packed away and the room is quiet once more, the mom examines the room, looks out the window, and knows that she has not done it perfectly, but she has walked with her God. He has sustained her. She's filled with anxious questions and a sad heart but also deep peace and rejoicing. Christ has been with her all the way, and he will be with her now and to the end. It turns out she's not just a Gospel Mom; she's a gospel woman. She's fully his and has a purpose still to serve. The only one she will continue to follow is him.

We know we're only a bit into this motherhood journey, but we can already tell that we're going to need more than the hope of raising perfect kids and achieving our idea of a good mom. We're going to need the one who is fully and utterly good and can make us good too. We know that we need to be united with Christ and let his life and words define, guide, correct, and comfort us all the way.

What kind of moms are we going to be? Gospel Moms.

WHAT KIND
OF MOMS
ARE WE
GOING TO BE?

GOSPEL
MOMS.

PART 1

THE FRAMEWORK

DISCOVERING A FRAMEWORK
FOR ALL OF LIFE

hen we were mothers with young children, we had a lot of questions about our daily decisions and circumstances. It felt like every ideal of, opinion on, and method for child-rearing we ever had was on the table and up for discussion. *How exactly do we sift through and implement all of this research and advice on so little sleep and still glorify God?* It seemed our entire world turned upside down, and we didn't know who to listen to in order to get it right side up. Though we followed Christ, we still felt like we faced an identity crisis, and we weren't quite sure who we were and what we stood for. It was in this season that we reached out to each other and began to talk about how being parents made our relatively steady ground feel shaky. We started asking each other about God's design for motherhood and how to discover it for ourselves. *Maybe if we know what God cares about, we'll know what to care about too.*

We went through a lot of back-and-forth. Correction and righting. Revising and amending. Because we lived five hours away from each other, we talked on the phone, asking each other questions about daily happenings—TV, snack time, that dreaded hour of crying before dinner—and discussing philosophical topics like discipline, creating fun, and how to explain suffering and sadness in a way our kids could understand. Over time, we recognized a pattern repeating in our conversations. We knew that God created the world for goodness, his world was broken by sin, Jesus came to fix what humanity broke, and one day, everything would be made right. From inconsolable babies to living with disabilities, every dilemma seemed subject to a good design, a broken reality, a right order, and a promised perfection. Later, we discovered we were going through a common thought process with established labels—Creation, Fall, Redemption, and Consummation. We spent time understanding the framework further, and it began to form the foundation for thinking through virtually any topic. It gave us a lens to see each situation in motherhood through. We haven't left it behind since.

This pattern tells the story of God redeeming our sin-wrecked world. Seeing how everything aligns to the one story God unfolds throughout history and in his world helped us clarify so many of our questions about what it means to be a Gospel Mom *and* how to act like a Gospel Mom. So we are turning to it once again as the foundation for this book. Over the next few chapters, we want to give you a primer on the framework that's helped shape our motherhood and the premise for this book.

Creation / Fall / Redemption / Consummation
Chapter 1

We'll explore how to discover God's created design for you in his Word so you can apply biblical principles to your own decisions and circumstances, asking, *How did God originally intend or design this to be?*

Chapter 2

We'll learn about and acknowledge the realities of the Fall so we can see how they might impact our current situation, asking, *How have sin and brokenness caused a divergence from God's original design?*

Chapter 3

We'll discover what was accomplished in redemption so we can keep the good news of Jesus Christ at the center as it transforms our hearts and thoughts, asking, *How can we rest in the work of Christ on the cross, walk by the Spirit, and obey God's teachings in this area of life?*

Chapter 4

We'll look forward to the hope of consummation and consider how its eternal promise gives us hope and meaning in our current circumstances, asking, *How does the assurance of future hope in eternity change my perspective, giving me renewed faith, clearer purpose, and a bigger mission today?*

We've chosen a high-level presentation of each step that we hope will give you a jump start on the topic while also allowing you to continue asking questions and searching for answers about biblical truth. As we go through each piece of the framework, we're going to focus on the pillar truths of the Christian faith versus the areas where Christians have a greater degree of disagreement. And we'll show you where we look to discover God's good design for life, the implications of living in a broken world, the realities of the promises of Christ that you have access to right this very moment, and how the hope of heaven transforms your life today.

Like the two of us when we started Risen Motherhood, you may be wondering, "How do I figure out what God's design is for my motherhood? I love God, I want to follow God, I want to do what he says, I want to be in his will…but I have no idea how to do that!"

While it's tempting to root our answers in our own experiences, the most recent research, a survey of our closest friends, or even the ideas of our favorite Bible teacher, it's important that we go to the Word of God itself *first* for insight and answers. Gospel Moms aren't loyal to a lifestyle, method, or stereotype, remember? The Bible is comprehensive and true and perfect—it's timeless and trustworthy for all our questions. Before we look for answers in the general revelation of God seen in the world around us—sometimes called the "Book of Nature"—let's first consider the many ways we can uncover God's design through the specific revelation in his Word, or the "Book of Scripture."

These first chapters may feel a bit abstract, information heavy even, but developing the foundational concept that informs gospel motherhood leads us to a more concrete understanding of being a Gospel Mom. Gospel motherhood isn't a quick fix, a fad, or another formula; it's a lifelong way of thinking and living.

To help make the connection between concepts and reality, we've added a section at the end of each of these four chapters called "You Can Do This," which describes a few of our go-to questions for understanding each topic. If you're eager to learn more or desire ways to learn to examine your own motherhood through this lens, we encourage you to check out *Becoming a Gospel Mom*, which includes even more questions and helps you dig deeper into these concepts.

More than a decade into motherhood, the questions haven't slowed down, only morphed and changed as our children have aged. Each week, we still discuss questions in motherhood and wonder how they match up to God's design, whether it's asking what roles we should play in our children's schools, how many hours to spend on income-producing work, what therapies to enroll our children with disabilities in, or how to walk with our children through the questions puberty brings. As mothers, it seems we're in a perpetual state of seeking God's will for our daily decisions and actions. We've learned to be comfortable with that.

Every day we seek him. Every day we think about how the concepts of Creation, Fall, Redemption, and Consummation play into the questions and circumstances we're facing. Every day we grow to be more like him. We have found the pursuit of Christ and his ways to be more worthwhile than anything else in our lives, because the gospel changes everything.

We promise you can do this too, Mom. Ready? Let's go.

CHAPTER 1

CREATION

Have you ever used a product that was impeccably designed? For Laura, it's her minivan. The Lord knew a mom's hands would always be full, and those automatic sliding doors are a gift straight from heaven. For Emily, it's her trusty all-terrain stroller she's used for a decade (with five kids) that's so well-encrusted in drool and snacks it's nearly petrified. For you, maybe it's a specific sleep sack that finally helped your baby sleep through the night. Maybe a certain lunch box solved all your packing headaches, keeping everything separate for a picky eater. Why did you fall in love with that product? Because of its good design. You felt like the designer thought of *everything*—providing a product that combined function, beauty, and purpose. They anticipated and met your needs, even some you didn't know you had.

The importance of good design is easy to spot when it comes to products, but what about when it comes to God's good design for life? For womanhood or motherhood or marriage? For work or friendships? That kind of good design is a bit harder to uncover and define. Yet that's exactly the type of question we need to ask if we're going to be Gospel Moms. When you know God's design for humanity, you will not just begin to understand how to spend your days as a mom, but you will also find freedom as you walk in faith in the unique circumstances God has given you. So in this chapter, we'll start with a quick overview of the creation story and then look at the implications of it for our lives. We'll see that there is a good designer, he only designs good things, he keeps us within his abundant goodness, and his goodness can be found all around us.

In the Beginning, God Created

The Bible opens with God creating. The Spirit of God hovers over the earth, and in a moment, God speaks the world into existence. The creation story isn't meant to be a science report, fit for peer review and publishing. It's a perfectly true account, poetically told so that we would know the origin of the earth and all that's in it. Genesis 1–2 doesn't tell us dates and times or answer all of our nitty-gritty questions (and it wasn't meant to), but it does point us to the creator himself and the goodness of all he made. He forms the earth and creates day and night, light and dark. He separates the water from the dry ground, creating habitable places for his creatures to live. He fills the heavens with celestial bodies, and he fills the sky, the water, and the ground with plant and animal life. Reading the story of his handiwork should invoke awe. Mountains pierce the sky, and their rock faces meet the home of whales and eels and kelp. Everything is abundant, creative, and unique, from flower varieties to types of fur. Animals crawl and slither, bound and climb. Some buzz, others roar. Every square inch is a treasure to behold, a reason to worship. And God makes it all good.

The pinnacle of God's creation was humankind, male and female, bearing the image of the creator. God placed them in the garden in Eden, designed them to be partners with God and each other, and blessed them to be fruitful and multiply and fill the earth as they worked together to see God's purposes carried out. Adam and Eve, the man and woman God created in the garden, had a perfect and intimate relationship with him. They lived in his presence and had conversations with him. They loved him and knew the feeling of his face shining upon them. Adam's and Eve's hearts beat for the things of God. Their desires matched his, and they worked in the world the way he had planned. God was glad to direct them and gave them clarity about his design—they could eat fruit from any tree except the one called the tree of the knowledge of good and evil. Otherwise, they could simply enjoy each other, the fullness of creation, and the work God had given them to do.

This origin story describes a world without the sin and brokenness we experience today. An ideal place where relationships were whole, fellowship with God and each other was sweet and shame-free, and work was full of reward and purpose. The creation story is the place to start when we try to determine God's intention for his people. It's in this story that we find key principles about how to view the world God made and our purpose within it.

There Is One Designer

As we consider God's intentions for our lives, it's important for us to acknowledge him as the absolute creator, designer, and Lord behind the blueprint for life. If we brush past these unchanging truths, we might be tempted to disregard aspects of his design that we don't immediately like or that don't fit into our culture's dominant worldview. Without God as our Lord, we'll be tempted to think of ourselves as the designers and, over time, we may change the definition of what is good, true, and beautiful.

For instance, we can see in Genesis 1–2 that God designed the concept of motherhood when he created Adam and Eve—and that he declared it very good. The first woman had a body that was made to do many things, including holding and nurturing a baby in her womb. Her breasts were designed to nourish her child's life. Her desire to bring forth children and see them raised to walk with God and do purposeful work on the earth was very good. As moms, when we hear the clamor of the culture, we might start to think that motherhood is a burden—something to be avoided, something to enter but hold at arm's length, or something to cling tightly to as our main identity and purpose in life. But if we acknowledge that God is the origin and sole designer of humankind, that we are merely stewards of all he has entrusted into our care—even our own children—we'll see that it's his opinion of motherhood that truly matters. When we understand this, we tune back into God's story of creation to see what he intended. Thankfully, God's opinion of motherhood and his overarching purpose for motherhood don't shift and change over time.

God Only Designs for Our Good

As you seek to understand and discover God's design for motherhood, believing that his way is the ultimate truth and the best way, you'll need to mine many parts of Scripture. God's intention for creation wasn't that humankind would have the bare minimum for survival. It's not as if humans were in a manufacturing plant of widgets, going through a uniform process to output uniform products, or as if humans were robots, coldly responding to a creator's coding in a barren land. Instead, his design includes untold beauty, truth, creativity, storytelling, and diversity. Just as Eden was a rich and luscious garden full of God's presence and delights for his creatures to enjoy, God invites us into life abundant as we walk in fellowship with him and seek to follow his commands.

This abundance mentality is also true in the way God presents his designs and intentions for creation throughout the Bible. He doesn't just give us a bulleted list of rules to live by in the first chapter of the Bible. The Bible isn't primarily a rule book (although God certainly does give plenty of important precepts and commands for us to heed). It's a book about him, his people, and the overarching rescue story that he's writing for his glory. Because of this, across all of Scripture he illustrates, weaves, commands, and gives pictures of what it means to submit to and follow him. While this can make uncovering his design for our lives feel a little more cumbersome at times or less straightforward, it also gives us an incredible opportunity to walk with him by faith as we study his Word with a desire to know and follow his ways.

A more extensive look at uncovering God's design in different sections of Scripture can be found in the companion workbook, *Becoming a Gospel*

Mom, but here are a few ways we can find God's good design for our lives throughout Scripture.

We Can Observe Israel

The narrative sections of the Old Testament give a historical account of Israel. The Pentateuch is the first five books of the Old Testament—also known as the Torah, which means "law" or "instruction." Written by Moses, these books tell the story of creation, to God's call of Abraham, all the way through the story of Israel becoming a nation. The Old Testament also includes books such as Joshua, Kings, and Esther, that continue the account of the people of Israel as they interacted with other nations. We know the Old Testament can feel difficult to understand at times, but Jesus said the Scriptures bore witness to him, which illustrates their importance and relevance to the Christian life.[1] When we read these narratives about God's people, we should consider how they point to Christ, God's design, and God's intentions for the world, especially in light of what we know from the New Testament.

We Can Get Wisdom

Wisdom literature includes Job, Psalms, Proverbs, Ecclesiastes, and Song of Songs. These books give numerous principles for godly living that help us make wise choices. We find warnings about things that are dangerous and encouragements to embrace what is good. These books aren't collections of hard-and-fast rules and regulations, but they do give us poetic insight into godly wisdom and decision-making and what God says is beneficial, harmful, or even deadly for his people.

We Can Listen to the Prophets

"The law and the prophets" were the writings that the Jewish people had up to the time of Christ, and Scripture tells us that they were all critical to

---

[1] John 5:39.

the full understanding of salvation and grace. These include books like Isaiah, Jeremiah, Daniel, Micah, and Jonah. Jesus actually spent time interpreting these Scriptures and helping his disciples understand how the prophets were speaking about the story of redemption, ultimately foreshadowing his life, death, resurrection, and final coming.[2] Some of the imagery can be hard to interpret and understand, and grasping the meaning of each prophet's words takes careful study. As we read the prophets, we learn about God's character and heart for his people, the architecture of redemption, his future plan for the church, and his design for heaven.

We Can Go Through the Gospels

In the Gospels, we read firsthand accounts of Jesus's life and ministry along with his trial, death, and resurrection. The Gospels include Matthew, Mark, Luke, and John. Later in the New Testament, we're told that we should walk as Jesus walked and our goal is to grow in our Christlikeness.[3] We see that he is the forerunner, the One who goes before us and the One we should emulate.[4] Studying the Gospels helps us form a solid understanding of what Jesus was like—how he treated others, what he prioritized and cared about, and how he obeyed the Father. We can also find ourselves in the stories of the disciples, Pharisees, tax collectors, and other Jews and Gentiles. We read of their doubts, their faith, what they got right, and what they got wrong, which brings both comfort and conviction. In the Gospels, as we listen to Jesus's words and observe his life, we discover a tangible model of God's design for our lives and how we should walk in his ways, making disciples and loving others.

We Can Gaze at the Early Church

Looking at the early church, including the letters and other accounts in

---

[2] Luke 24:27; 24:4.

[3] 1 John 2:6; John 14:21; 2 Corinthians 3:18.

[4] Hebrews 6:20.

the New Testament, also helps us uncover God's plan. In books like Acts, James, and Hebrews, we learn about God's design for the church: its structure, its purpose, and its mission. In many of the Epistles (the letters to the early church), we also find instructions for marriage and family and the way we are to relate to one another as members of the body of Christ. We learn about the trials and tribulations that Christians might face as they live in the world and spread the gospel, but we also see the hope and comfort available as we patiently endure.

We Can Understand the End

We can uncover God's design by looking ahead in the book of Revelation and some parts of prophetic literature, like the book of Daniel. These parts of Scripture give us an idea of what things are going to look like someday, including Christ's return, the fulfillment of all God's promises, and God's final judgment. In particular, Revelation is prophetic and apocalyptic literature, offering an unveiling of a future reality through symbols as John records visions given to him by God. Even though it's still shrouded in tremendous mystery, Revelation provides us with a picture of what we're all hoping for and holding on to. Here we can discover more about God's perfect design for his people and his ultimate purpose for our world and mankind into eternity.

Boundaries Keep Us in Pleasant Places

What we learn as we read through and study Scripture is that God's designs are a lot like the boundaries we give our children for their safety and, ultimately, for their joy. At the park, we use landmarks like "Don't go past that tree or that fence!" And it's not because we're mean or restrictive—we give boundaries because we want our children to have fun and enjoy their time at the park. We want them to be safe. Whether or not they see it or comprehend it, the parking lot is past the tree, and the road is past the fence. As their loving mom, we surveyed the landscape and laid boundary lines for their good and enjoyment. Now they just need to trust us and obey! The same is true when children get older and we set boundaries for apps, websites, and videos or set a curfew. We're not being killjoys; we're being loving mothers with a plan for our children's highest good.

In many ways, the same is true of God's plan for his children. The things that are best for us both now and in eternity are the things that God laid out in Scripture. He is a loving Father who wants to keep his children safe and near—to see them have abundant and thriving lives, full of joy and purpose. He's not a Father who draws arbitrary boundaries just to keep his children from having fun or getting the most out of life on this earth. God is good, he's the ultimate designer, and his design is always the best possible thing for our lives.

We know this is true because of the abundant goodness God provided for Adam and Eve in the garden, and we see it illustrated in his clear command and protection that they not eat from the tree of the knowledge of good and evil. God's one boundary wasn't just keeping them from a sweet bite of fruit that they might enjoy; it was keeping them from separation, shame, broken relationships, guilt, and ultimately death and banishment from the garden. When we begin to doubt God's intentions for our good in his commands or we start to wonder, *Did God really say?* we can go back to the creation story and see his heart for his children.

Creation Testifies to God's Good Design

Not only does God help us uncover his good design in the Bible itself, but he also helps us understand it through the world he made and how it works. In the "Book of Nature," as some call it, God has given general revelation through creation, tradition, reason, and experience. His created design for the world did not disappear when sin entered. Sin tainted it, but our merciful God left his fingerprints on all that we encounter. All things must be tested against Scripture, as it's our ruling authority, but we can take things we learn through science, psychology, sociology, church tradition and history, our friends, our own life experience, and more and consider them contributions to our deepening understanding of God's design. Wisdom found

THE THINGS
THAT ARE BEST
FOR US BOTH
NOW AND IN
ETERNITY ARE
THE THINGS
THAT GOD
LAID OUT IN
SCRIPTURE.

in God's creation isn't restricted to research or advice given by other believers either. In his common grace and goodness, God allows any person—in 2 Samuel, he even uses a donkey—to sometimes understand and clearly communicate aspects of his design, which means we can learn from their research and knowledge.

Looking to the Book of Nature is particularly helpful as we ask questions that the Bible doesn't make direct claims about. Things like: *How does God intend for us to handle specific technologies? What is the ideal way to help someone through a mental illness? What are the best-known ways to treat disease?* In this book, we're not able to get into many specifics, but here are a few ways we can learn from the Book of Nature:

- Observe people and their relationships with God and one another, gleaning principles for healthy relationships.

- Learn about how to interpret Scripture and live as a bold believer from Christians who've stood the test of time and maintained orthodox church history.

- Observe nature—learning about God as we admire the intricacies of a flower petal, marveling at the patterns and the animals God has made, and so on.

- Glean information from good scientific research, published studies, and those who are experts in their fields.

- Be moved to a greater understanding of the story of redemption as we encounter good stories and testimonies in our lives.

- Gain ideas for how to handle past trauma or painful experiences in our lives from counselors and therapists.

- Receive help from traditional medical doctors and naturopathic physicians for ailments.

- Allow artistic works and words to communicate something about the way the world is and how we're meant to exist in it.

- Listen to the teaching and wisdom of pastors, elders, and Christian leaders and mentors.

An important note: God's Word is rooted in a certain time and place, but the truths within are timeless. God didn't hold back anything he wanted to tell us in Scripture; the big ideas and principles are clear. So if he didn't make an issue abundantly clear in his Word, like the specific methods and means of living his will, then we don't need to get too worked up playing detective about God's detailed boundary lines in every area of modern life. As we are trying to understand what is right and good and true, we can pair a deep biblical grounding, led by the Holy Spirit, with life experience and learn more about God's design for his people in the many different times and places and with the many unique issues facing his people.

You Can Do This!

As we look in the Word and at the world around us, God's good design for life will begin to crystallize. It doesn't mean that life will work perfectly if we "do it all right." (Spoiler alert: We won't do it all right. Don't forget that we're studying the Fall in the next chapter!) But it gives us a good guide for what to aim for as we make both major life decisions and minor adjustments to our day-to-day lives.[5]

---

[5] For examples of how aspects of the gospel framework play out, you can see our first book, *Risen Motherhood: Gospel Hope for Everyday Moments.* In it, we take 16 topics common to motherhood and use personal scenarios to show how CFRC might play out in someone's real life.

Here are some questions you can ask yourself or your friends when you start to think through the lens of Creation:

1. How did God originally intend or design this to be?
2. How would it function without sin and brokenness?
3. How does it reflect the beauty of who God is?
4. Where does Scripture address this topic and the ways God has designed it to flourish?

One question we tend to come back to over and over is this: What principles, standards, or truths have remained for all people for all of time? We'll dig into this more in part 3, but this is a great question to help define what God values and expects of his people.

As Gospel Moms, we know God has a good design for our lives. We know we won't always get it right or understand every detail of how things should perfectly be, but we trust him and believe his ways are supremely wise and for our good. He gives us pleasant boundary lines for flourishing, and we can know what they are. God has not held out on us. He's given us all that he wants us to know in his Word, through creation, and by the help of the Holy Spirit living inside us. He is our King. We are loyal always, only, to him.

GOD'S DESIGN IS ALWAYS THE BEST POSSIBLE THING FOR OUR LIVES.

CHAPTER 2

FALL

L ong before we reached motherhood, we already had a deep sense of knowing life on earth isn't perfect. But motherhood seems to shine a bright spotlight on life's imperfections— we see it in our friend's grief over a miscarriage, in our own struggles with being patient or kind, and in our children's disobedience. As moms, we shiver with fear hearing stories of child abuse or watching a friend's teenager struggle with suicidal ideation. We can't believe a child in our kids' class really goes without meals over the weekend. And we feel the dissonance in our own lives too. We see it on a tired Monday morning when we can't muster up a cheerful voice as we hurry to get our kids off to school. We feel it when we wipe the kitchen counters for the seventh time that day. We know it when we take our child to a doctor's appointment and they tell us we need to order a scan.

We spent the last chapter talking about the creation story and God's original design for flourishing, but all of us know we don't live that reality. People who seem to be following Jesus are still selfish and make decisions that cause harm. Even those who have money, resources, talents, and gifts eventually realize they can't strong-arm life and make it go according to their plans. That's because we live on a planet infiltrated with sin and brokenness. In order to apply the next section of the gospel framework—the Fall—we'll look at what events brought sin into God's sinless creation and how they impacted the storyline of humanity, then spend the rest of our time considering the Fall's implications on our lives, discussing how it impacts our hearts, relationships, the earth, and our bodies.

What Happened to Our World?

Genesis moves from displaying God's original design for creation to telling the story of the Fall. The garden God had placed Adam and Eve in was a magnificent display of his creativity, goodness, and artistry. From orchards and forests to flowers and fruits, Eden dazzled with newly planted life and beauty. Wide, flowing rivers teemed with newly created abundance and animals. It was a masterpiece—and God wasn't even done.[1] God intended for Adam and Eve to partner with him to expand the glories of the garden as the glory of God covered the whole earth. Yet Eden was vulnerable, as humanity was still susceptible to sin. While God gave them the entire garden to care for and enjoy, God also warned Adam and Eve in Genesis 2:17 of one forbidden tree—the tree of the knowledge of good and evil—and how "in the day that you eat of it you shall surely die."[2]

While we can only imagine a garden of every good thing, Adam and Eve walked in it day in and day out. They spent time with God, learning and enjoying this perfect place of provision, and yet they were still lured in by the lies and temptations of a creature that spoke against the God they intimately knew. The Gospel of Luke helps us understand that the serpent who approached Adam and Eve was Satan, a fallen angel who was cast out of heaven because of his rebellion.[3] After Eve's conversation with the snake, she thought he had a point—maybe there was a better way of life than what God designed. So surrounded by every good fruit from the hand of God, she took a bite of the only one he had forbidden. Then she turned to hand it to

---

[1] Genesis 2:8.

[2] Genesis 2:17.

[3] Luke 10:18; Revelation 12:9.

Adam as well. Genesis records the rebellion, saying, "The woman saw that the tree was good for food and delightful to look at, and that it was desirable for obtaining wisdom. So she took some of its fruit and ate it; she also gave some to her husband, who was with her, and he ate it."[4]

God hadn't given them a gray area. He was clear, direct, and straightforward: "Do not eat." But Adam and Eve did it anyway. Genesis 3 records their treason, and it also records the fallout. Sin entered the world when the forbidden fruit entered their bodies and then spread like a virus.

After the disastrous bite, Adam and Eve possessed exactly what God said they would: the knowledge of good and evil. They became "wise," knowing sin and sadness for the very first time. Suddenly their nakedness brought a flush to their cheeks, as their sin brought on feelings of shame. They hid in the bushes, aware that they now stood unholy before a holy God. Ashamed and afraid, they heard God coming, looking for the people he loved. God wasn't just out for a stroll, whistling while enjoying the fresh air. God was aware of what happened, and he was on a mission to talk with Adam and Eve. Disobedience would surely bring divine judgment.

God approaches Adam and Eve and asks, "What is this that you have done?"[5] While Adam gets defensive and blames Eve, Eve squirms and blames the serpent, both of them pointing fingers for the broken covenant in every direction but themselves. In response, God curses the serpent and the ground. He tells Eve that she will experience pain in bearing and raising children, that her desire will be for her husband but he will rule over her, and that Adam will struggle and toil over the ground.[6]

God warns them: sin equals death. Adam and Eve couldn't have fathomed the extent of this destruction. Death crept in, somehow both slow and sudden. Their previously uncorrupted bodies would decline. Adam and

---

[4] Genesis 3:6 CSB.

[5] Genesis 3:13.

[6] Genesis 3:16-19.

Eve would begin to experience the first realities of aging, which would lead to their eventual physical deaths. Their once healthy hearts would now harbor a sickness.

But divine judgment comes with divine mercy. God promises the new chapter of history they just entered won't be the final chapter—he will send an offspring or a "seed" that will ultimately crush Satan, defeat death, and restore God's people. God provides animal skins for Adam and Eve to replace their flimsy fig leaf coverings, which gives them their first look at what would become a regular practice: the slaughter of animals as a picture of innocent blood given for the guilty. This atoning covering symbolizes the need for someone to take the punishment for sin. It is a picture of God's promise to provide a way back to him.

Now Adam and Eve can no longer be in the presence of a holy God, and they have to leave the garden. God knows if they eat from another special tree in the garden, the tree of life, they will remain in their sinful state for eternity. Out of an abundance of love and protection, he banishes them from the garden. We can hear the determined love in his voice when we read the words,

> Then the LORD God said, "…Now, lest [the man] reach out his hand and take also of the tree of life and eat, and live forever—" therefore the LORD God sent him out from the garden of Eden to work the ground from which he was taken. He drove out the man, and at the east of the garden of Eden he placed the cherubim and a flaming sword that turned every way to guard the way to the tree of life.[7]

The Far-Reaching Effects of the Fall

This is quite a change from the content of our last chapter, where we rejoiced in and discovered God's good design, isn't it? Just three chapters

---

[7] Genesis 3:22-24.

into the Bible, things take a serious turn. It feels like the middle of a fairy tale, where everything goes wrong and you don't quite know how the characters will be rescued by the hero. While, thankfully, we live on this side of redemption, and Scripture does tell us how we are rescued—that's discussed in the next two chapters of this book—the Fall brought sin, suffering, evil, and shame into the world, and we live with all of that today. In order to understand our lives and relationships with God and others, we need to look for the fingerprints of the Fall on our hearts, our motherhood, and the world around us.

There are many ways to think about the effects of the Fall, but it's probably easiest if we break it down into four main categories: the effects of the Fall on our hearts, on our relationships, on the earth, and on our bodies.

The Effects of the Fall on Our Hearts

Sin is in all our hearts. In the Bible, sin is defined as breaking the law of God, failing to do what God has required, and rebelling against God.[8] It's any feeling, will, or thought originating in the human heart that doesn't value God above all things.[9] The Bible tells us we have all inherited a sin nature from Adam. Romans 5:12 tells us that because of one man's sin (Adam's), we've all sinned.[10] And Romans 3:23 says, "All have sinned and fall short of the glory of God." In the Psalms, King David laments about how he was sinful at birth—sinful from the time his mother conceived him.[11] We're all prone to evil, "by nature children of wrath."[12]

Sin is not just something we do; it's who we are until we are made new in Christ. Apart from God, we are in bondage to sin, resistant to the goodness and light that comes from him: "The mind that is set on the flesh is hostile

---

[8] 1 John 3:4; Deuteronomy 9:7; Joshua 1:18.

[9] In biblical language, the heart refers to the desires of our souls. It's the seat of our emotions, love, and will.

[10] Romans 5:12.

[11] Psalm 51:5.

[12] Ephesians 2:3.

to God, for it does not submit to God's law; indeed, it cannot."[13] Because we have inherited a sin nature from Adam, we can't escape the guilt and punishment for sin apart from Jesus. Even after we have been rescued through Christ's redemption, sin is still a battle for believers until we reach heaven.

As Jesus is speaking to the disciples, he tells them that sin springs from the heart: "But the things that proceed out of the mouth come from the heart, and those defile the man. For out of the heart come evil thoughts, murders, adulteries, fornications, thefts, false witness, slanders."[14] Jeremiah 17:9 says, "The heart is deceitful above all things, and desperately sick; who can understand it?" Sin occurs when our hearts don't treasure God above all; instead, we willfully pick something else to reign supreme in our hearts. Our children, our homes, our reputations, our husbands, our physical appearance, our income-producing work—the options are limitless when it comes to what the human heart can place first on the throne.

At times we are all tempted to make light of sin and say, "Oh, I'm just misbehaving or up to a bit of mischief." No, sin is a deep offense against a holy God. The Bible uses strong words to describe sin, calling it *transgression, rebellion, adultery, a trespass, going astray,* and *being unfaithful.* These are big, alarming words that we have to suffer with when we talk about the Fall.

While sin in our hearts affects more than just our behaviors, it can be helpful to identify sin in two main groups: sins of action and sins of inaction.

Sins of action. Most of us, when we think about sin or wrongdoing, think about things we *actually do.* The theological term for this is a "sin of commission." Humanity's first sin was a sin of commission, as Adam and Eve knew God's command to not eat from the tree of the knowledge of good and evil, and yet they blatantly and deliberately disobeyed. Most sins of commission are obvious, like stealing or lying. Other things can feel up to debate—*Is it gossip to discuss another mom's parenting methods at book club, or*

---

[13] Romans 8:7.

[14] Matthew 15:18-19 NASB.

SIN OCCURS WHEN OUR HEARTS DON'T TREASURE GOD ABOVE ALL.

is it just observing and sharing information? Where's the line? Still, others can be easy to hide or ignore, like envious thoughts over another mom's home. These sins can be intentional or unintentional, but nevertheless, they are sins. They are often more than we are even able to see or recognize at one time. In these kinds of sins, we perform an action in our hearts or with our bodies that reveals our rejection of God in exchange for something else—control, power, prestige, comfort, and more.

Sins of inaction. We can also sin by not doing the good we should do. Theologically, these are called "sins of omission," as they are sins of *inaction*. The word *sin* is a Greek archery term that describes any shot that doesn't hit the bull's-eye. Sin literally means missing the mark. James writes, "So whoever knows the right thing to do and fails to do it, for him it is sin."[15] Sins of omission can also be intentional or unintentional. Sometimes they can feel impossible and overwhelming to grapple with, and at other times they are more subtle and sneaky to identify. For instance, God commands us to love our neighbor, but we don't always love all of our neighbors to the highest degree that we could or should. We miss opportunities to do good to others, like listening and showing compassion to a friend in her parenting dilemma, or we don't listen to the Spirit's prompting to bring that struggling new mom a meal. God says to love the poor, to be generous, to do good to one another, to speak truth, and to be gracious—but we don't always do these things. A sin of omission is not doing something we should. Even if we haven't done a lot of obvious "bad things," we still haven't perfectly and wholly loved the Lord our God with all our heart, soul, mind, and strength or done all the right or good things.[16]

Our Sin Breaks Relationships

If you've been a mom for any number of years, you'll likely have heard

---

[15] James 4:17.

[16] Deuteronomy 6:5; Luke 10:27.

of the "mommy wars." It's a loosely used term to describe mothers dividing up into factions and "going to war" with other moms over their beliefs on the best ways to raise children. Whole books have been written on why certain ways of mothering are the best ways and why all the others are wrong. Blogs, social media platforms, and forums can be found around the internet encouraging one way of thinking and decrying all the others, telling us the other camps are (at best) misguided and (at worst) harmful, unloving, or even abusive. There tends to be little tolerance between tribes, each driving a flag in a method to claim it as superior. These wars are even happening in Christian mom culture today as we divide over lifestyle choices and motherhood methodologies. Like the early church, we have "jealousy and strife" among us, with some saying, "'I follow Paul,' and another, 'I follow Apollos,'" when we really should all just be following Christ.[17]

Whether it's a discipline method, a sleep-training technique, your policy on Santa, your thoughts on if moms should or shouldn't work outside the home, or your philosophy on phones, the mommy wars shine a spotlight on what has happened to all of humanity since our exit from Eden. We saw it immediately in the garden when Eve blamed the serpent and Adam blamed Eve for their catastrophic decision. The arrival of sin broke relationships horizontally, person to person, causing jealousies, strife, misunderstandings, and judgments. But sin also broke the vertical relationship: our relationship with God. Isaiah 59:1-2 says, "Behold, the LORD's hand is not shortened, that it cannot save, or his ear dull, that it cannot hear; but your iniquities have made a separation between you and your God, and your sins have hidden his face from you so that he does not hear."

Sin broke our relationship with God. Every sin, whether committed against someone else or privately on our own, is an offense against our holy God—breaking our "vertical relationship" with him. When we think about this, it's important we understand that when we refer to God's holiness,

---

[17] 1 Corinthians 3:3-4.

we're summarizing his entire, unfathomable moral perfection in one word. Sin is absolutely appalling and horrific to God—it's a cosmic betrayal against the King of the universe. We can't simply say, "Whoops, I messed up." Sin is a huge transgression—so huge it always requires atonement. As we saw in Genesis 3, before God cast Adam and Eve out of the garden, he slaughtered an animal and made clothing for Adam and Eve. This may have been the first death, the first blood Adam and Eve had ever seen spilled. Imagine the horror they must have felt when they realized that an innocent animal died for them, in their place. It's a picture that we often forget: Sin is an evil transgression against a holy God, and it always leads to death.

Sin broke our relationship with others. Immediately after their fatal bite of fruit, Adam and Eve went from lovers to enemies, pointing fingers and placing blame. We see in their relationship how quickly sin can break our "horizontal relationships" with others. We often think of sin against others in really big ways—things like murder, rape, war, and adultery. The first major scene is right after Adam and Eve are cast out of the garden, when one of Eve's sons murders her other son out of envy. (Can you imagine the crushing heartbreak as a mother?) But sin also reveals itself in smaller ways, like when we conceal our shopping from our husbands or when we burst out in anger toward our children. It clouds our views and leads to misconceptions about people's motives or wrong assumptions about what they said or did. In all of it, sin breaks God's original design of harmony in community.

This is a lot of discussion around sin. It's heavy and can be hard to read. But hang in there! We're going to talk about two more ways the Fall has affected our lives outside of sin, which will help explain many of the sorrows and griefs you're facing in your own life. And the good news is a few pages away.

The Effects of the Fall on the Earth

In Genesis 3, God cursed the ground as a consequence for Adam and Eve's sin, changing the natural order of the world. Out of its Edenic state, our earth has a degenerative condition. As God details the curse on the ground to Adam

SIN BREAKS GOD'S ORIGINAL DESIGN OF HARMONY IN COMMUNITY.

in the garden, he says, "Cursed is the ground because of you; in toil you will eat of it all the days of your life. Both thorns and thistles it shall grow for you; and you will eat the plants of the field; by the sweat of your face you will eat bread, till you return to the ground."[18] In Romans 8:20-21, Paul writes about how the Fall affected all of creation, using phrases like being *subjected to frustration*, having *bondage to decay*, and *needing liberation*.

Now we have natural disasters like floods, tornadoes, wildfires, and droughts wreaking havoc on our homes and lands. We face daily difficulties like weeds in our vegetable gardens, leaks in our kitchen faucets, sunburns from being outside too long, and hail damage to our roofs. These things are not sins, but they are a consequence of the Fall, and they make life harder than God originally designed it.

Now we face endless piles of laundry with stains we can't remove no matter how much we scrub. We face formula shortages and cannot feed our babies. Basements flood, and we face expensive bills to fix the damage. It is a life of "thorns and thistles" where we can never truly get ahead. Understanding the curse offers an explanation for why things don't operate the way they should. It gives a reason for many of the painful realities we experience today that our own mothers might say are "just a part of life!" While that doesn't necessarily make doing another load of laundry less tiresome, it helps us understand the realities of the world we exist in.

The Effects of the Fall on Our Bodies

God crafted our physical being, and when the son of God came to humanity, he took on a body. This means bodies matter to God. We are embodied beings, and what happens to our physical bodies has significance in our lives. We feel the pain of the Fall in our bodies. While sometimes the suffering in our bodies (or in the bodies of those we love) is due to a person's sin, more often than not, it's simply a reality of living on a broken earth. It's

---

[18] Genesis 3:17-19 NASB.

a result of death and decay being in the picture. Our bones break, our hair falls out, our toes stub, our skin gets cuts and scars. Now a mother's womb doesn't always carry a baby as long as it should—or even at all. Childbirth is painful and can be filled with questions, fear, and groaning. Breastfeeding isn't always possible. Our children are sometimes born with developmental delays or genetic abnormalities or are mute, deaf, or blind. Our own parents struggle with disease—cancer, Parkinson's, Alzheimer's—and need our attention and care. Mothers are susceptible to mental illness, with the possibility of postpartum depression (PPD), clinical depression, postpartum anxiety (PPA), and more as constant companions. Disfigurement, chronic illness, terminal illness, and disability all can affect our ability to function as moms. A mother's back might require surgery from carrying a child on her hip for years and years, her ankles may painfully swell from months of growing a life inside her womb, her body may become exhausted from weeks of insomnia at night.

And of course, now all of us face a clock from the day we are born, and someday, each of us will die. For some of our children, it will feel much too soon. For others, we will live many days and have what will be called a "good, long life." But it is still shorter than God's original design in the garden, where Adam and Eve could have known a life free of death. The struggles we face in our temporary dwellings are a real cause for grief and shouldn't be dismissed or downplayed. We're living in a legacy of death, and our bodies feel it.

Don't Give Up

Chances are, reading all that was a downer for you. But don't give up now! It's like when one of us recommends a show, movie, or book to the other and we suddenly find that the other person doesn't love it as much when they start it. We have to reassure the other that things get better in the next book, to keep watching for the sequel, and to know it will be worth it—this is just the beginning of a bigger story. The gospel framework can feel a little like that. We've never loved any story as much as the one God is telling, but this is the hard part we sometimes have to slog through to get to the rest. It's not the part we are supposed to love; it's the part that should push us forward to keep going and behold the work of the greatest storyteller of all time. From here we look to the promise that it will get better. We *will* like it more. So keep reading, knowing it will be worth it.

You Can Do This!

If this chapter has you feeling uncomfortable or sad, we understand. These are hard realities. As Gospel Moms, we long to live out God's design, but we have to grapple with the bad news in order to fully appreciate and understand the good news that's coming. It is okay and right to grieve the realities of the Fall. This life isn't the way it's supposed to be, and everything in you knows it. Here are some quick questions you can ask when you start to think through the lens of the Fall:

1. How has this situation or topic diverged from God's original design through the curse on the earth or my body?

2. How has sin infiltrated my thoughts, words, or actions, and how is it keeping me from living according to God's good plan?

3. Am I sinning by commission (doing something I shouldn't) or omission (not doing something I should)?

Remember that this isn't the end of the story. In the midst of all the devastation in Eden, God embeds a promise to our first parents (a mom and dad!) in his words to the serpent: "I will put enmity between you and the woman, and between your offspring and her offspring; he shall bruise your head, and you shall bruise his heel."[19] The serpent with the hissing lies will be crushed. Sin does not have the final word for us. It is no match for the saving work of God in Christ Jesus.

[19] Genesis 3:15.

CHAPTER 3

REDEMPTION

There were many questions to answer when we first explored the idea of starting a podcast: *What kind of microphones do we use? Where do we upload and distribute the audio? Once we hit record, what in the world do we say?* But most importantly, if we were going to air conversations about everyday issues of motherhood in light of the gospel, *what would we call it?* After a few brainstorming sessions, with more than a few hilariously bad ideas, Emily's husband (also Laura's brother) threw out a name that stuck: Risen Motherhood. We loved that because the word *risen* perfectly captures the part of the story that Christian moms are living in today. Though we still endure life after the Fall, we're living after Jesus Christ rose from the grave. As his followers, we have new life in him, and we mother with the expectation that we will rise to be with him again someday, too, when all is made right.

Resurrection should make us think of redemption. And redemption is the next part of the story we need to remember as Gospel Moms. We don't live a "fallen motherhood"—primarily focusing on all the ways that motherhood is sorrowful and hard, or shrugging off and ignoring our failures—we live in the Redemption part of the gospel framework, believing that God is working in and through the hard or sad things for his glory and we get to participate in it. Without the completed work of Christ to save us and all the implications of that salvation, we might still be able to learn about God's design and feel the weight of the Fall, but we'd be stuck in our own cliff-hanger—no hope, no resolution, no sequel, and no good news. Thankfully, that's not where God left us.

In this chapter, we're going to take time to explore exactly what redemption is and how it comes about in the story of Scripture, and we'll look into how the person and work of Christ begins to restore his people to his good design.

God Brought Redemption Through His Son

First, what is *redemption*? Redemption, in the simplest terms, is salvation from sin and death.

In the chapter on Creation, we talked about how God has a good design for his people and that he instructed Adam and Eve (and all his image bearers, for that matter) to live according to his commands, free of sin and full of trust and dependence on him. But as we learned in the previous chapter, Adam and Eve disobeyed God, and as a result, everyone falls short of the glory of God.[1] We left things on a low note, on the "bad news" that sin, death, and the curse impact every facet of life and creation. But as God promised all the way back in Genesis 3:15, that wouldn't be the final chapter of the story—he would send an offspring, or a "seed," that would ultimately crush Satan, defeat death, and restore God's people to himself. The work of salvation wouldn't be a work that his people would do—trying to earn their way back into his good graces—but it would be something he would do on their behalf. God promised an offspring who would be "bruised" and crushed but ultimately defeat our enemy, rescue us, and restore our relationship with God again.

The incredible thing about the promise of salvation at the beginning of the Bible is that it shows redemption wasn't an afterthought or an

---

[1] Romans 3:23.

emergency backup plan. The triune God has been full of perfect wisdom for all of time—from "before the beginning of the earth," as it says in Proverbs 8:22-23. "In the beginning," Jesus, the Word made flesh, was with God and was God.[2] And Scripture tells us that God "chose us in him before the foundation of the world, that we should be holy and blameless before him."[3] These verses, plus many other places throughout Scripture, assure us that though it is a wild mystery to us at times, redemption is God's best and most glorious plan for his creation and his people.

As the rest of the Old Testament unfolds, the promise of a Savior expands and grows with each generation of the story. When we read the story of the flood, Noah, and the ark, we learn the promised one to come is the ark that will bring us safely through death and God's ultimate judgment. When we read about God's people enslaved in Egypt, wiping the blood of a spotless lamb on their doorposts and trusting in God by faith that death would pass over them, we are being pointed to one whose blood covers us and saves us from eternal death and separation from God. Each book of the Old Testament moves history closer to the promised Savior while it displays what he will be like and what he will accomplish.

The New Testament opens with a genealogy, an announcement that the promised offspring has arrived. His name is Jesus, and he is fully human and fully divine—the very son of God born of a woman. Through his sinless life, death on the cross, and rising again, Christ achieved a full victory over sin and death. His victory secure, Jesus ascended to heaven to take his throne at the right hand of the Father. Right now, that's where he reigns and rules over the world. And while Jesus remains in heaven, Satan is allowed to operate and believers still struggle with sin and feel the effects of the Fall.[4]

But as Gospel Moms, because of his redemption, we're no longer subject

---

[2] John 1:1-14.

[3] Ephesians 1:4.

[4] Ephesians 2:2; Romans 7:15-20.

to the enemy's rule. We're citizens of heaven, we're part of God's kingdom, we're children of our Heavenly Father, we're filled with the Holy Spirit. Though we live in a world that can't find peace and rest, we get to live in the truth that Jesus has overcome the world, and in him, we can find peace even in hard circumstances.[5] We're expectantly waiting for the final chapter where God will make all things new, exercise his perfect justice, and dwell with his people for eternity.

Though most of you have heard the story of Jesus's life, death, and resurrection, you may not have stopped to think about all the pieces and why they matter to your actual life. When you think of the gospel framework, think of Redemption as the linchpin. Redemption is where everything changes, and it holds together what we're living in now and what we wait for in the future. Getting this under your skin is the part that will give you true freedom as you navigate your everyday decisions with joy. It all revolves around the person and work of Jesus Christ.

Jesus Was the Only Perfect Human

Scripture tells us that Jesus humbled himself when he came to earth as a man in order to save his people.[6] Jesus is God's only "begotten" son, born of the Virgin Mary through miraculous conception.[7] Jesus was and is fully God and fully man. This is hard for our human brains to understand, but it's true. In his birth to his earthly parents, Mary and Joseph, Jesus met all of the biblical requirements to be the promised Messiah and the one who sits on the throne of David forever. The way his birth and life took place perfectly fulfilled every prophecy about where he would be born and live and what his life would be like and accomplish.

But he wasn't just a man; he was a perfect man—uncorrupted. Though

---

[5] John 16:33.

[6] Philippians 2:8.

[7] Matthew 1:23.

Jesus can identify with our lived experience in his humanness, he was not born into sin. When faced with the frustrations, griefs, and challenges of life, he never complained, turned from God, or gave in to despair. He never disobeyed his parents or treated another human with anything short of perfect love. He fulfilled the law of Moses and lived as a perfect Jew, according to God's commands. He always did the exact right thing—being totally faithful to God and his mission.[8] We even learn that Jesus was tempted by Satan after 40 days in the wilderness without food and water, but in the deepest state of physical and mental weakness, he never gave in to offers of power and provision apart from his Father's hand.[9] Instead, he boldly claimed and clung to the truth of God's words and promises. This and many other instances prove that Jesus is pure, spotless, and blameless, without blemish or error in heart or action. We have all sinned and fallen short of the glory of God, but Jesus, being the "image of the invisible God," has never sinned and is the glory of God. He is due our worship in all his glory.[10]

Seeing Jesus as both the perfect human and very son of God helps us align our lives with God's intentions and good design:

We can understand true humility and go to our Savior for comfort. Jesus's incarnation gives us an understanding of God's love for us and a picture of what it means to humble ourselves and look to the interests of others. Jesus's experience of humanity assures us that he understands the many ways we struggle, experience temptation, feel grief, and walk in weakness. We can go to him and know that he sympathizes with us.

We don't strive for the world's definition of success and status. Jesus's lowly entrance into the world—born in a "nowhere" type of place and laid in an animal's feeding trough—shows that prestige and clout aren't what give us significance in the kingdom of God. Nor does it matter if we aren't socially

---

[8] 1 Peter 2:22; 1 John 3:5.

[9] Luke 4:1-13.

[10] Colossians 1:15.

influential, highly accomplished in our careers, financially wealthy, and so on. Isaiah 53:2 gives us a description of Jesus as a man: "For he grew up before him like a young plant, and like a root out of dry ground; he had no form or majesty that we should look at him, and no beauty that we should desire him." This verse shows us that culturally accepted standards of beauty aren't what determine our worth or value to God and the kingdom. The fact that Jesus was not too important for mundane work, spending much of his life as a carpenter before his public ministry, gives us great hope that all of our work matters to God and can bring glory to him, even as we live most of our days in the mundane.

We can have spiritual power to obey God, knowing we're fully righteous in Christ. When we turn from our sin and put our faith in Christ, God transfers Christ's perfect righteousness to us.[11] Acting righteously is now a privilege. We can look to Jesus's life as a perfect example of how to follow God, live faithfully, and love others. Though we don't live in the exact same time or culture as Jesus, we should obey him and emulate his life in our own relationships and circumstances. When we face temptation, we can call upon the same strength that sustained Christ. We won't be able to resist all sin in this life, but we can take heart knowing that his ability to resist sin and evil is infallible.

We can find the wisdom and answers we need. When we need to know what to do in a situation, we can trust the guidance of the Spirit through the life and words of Christ because we know they will be righteous, holy, and good.

Jesus Was the Only Perfect Sacrifice

The fact that Jesus was fully righteous and perfect is also what makes him the ultimate once-and-for-all-time sacrifice for sin.[12] He was falsely accused

---

[11] 1 Corinthians 1:30.

[12] Hebrews 10:12.

ALL OF OUR WORK MATTERS TO GOD AND CAN BRING GLORY TO HIM.

by religious leaders, unjustly tried and convicted, and sentenced to a death that he did not deserve. He was innocent. But we learn in Scripture that though he had the authority to break his bonds and demolish his persecutors there on the spot, he willingly went to the cross, taking the punishment of death we deserved and the wrath of God on our behalf: "He was pierced for our transgressions; he was crushed for our iniquities; upon him was the chastisement that brought us peace, and with his wounds we are healed."[13] As the spotless lamb, his death ended the need for the ongoing sacrificial system that the Jews adhered to. When Jesus said "It is finished" on the cross, he meant that our sins were fully and finally atoned for.[14]

And his death was fully and totally real. Jesus wasn't just *almost* dead on the cross. He was *dead* dead—no breath, no pulse, no physical life. His body was removed from the cross, ritually prepared for burial, put into a tomb, and sealed behind a giant stone that was stationed with a Roman guard. While we might be tempted to fast-forward through this part of the story, it's still important because Jesus's experience of bodily death, as his Spirit departed, is part of how we can be sure of his defeat over death.[15]

There are so many ways that Christ's death brings us life:

We're free from sin's penalty, guilt, and shame. When we're struggling with guilt or shame, we can remember that there is no more condemnation for those who are in Christ Jesus.[16] God has no more wrath for our sins! We can approach the throne of grace with confidence.[17] We don't try to do "good things" or live a certain way to earn God's favor or defer the punishment we fear we'll receive for doing something wrong. There is no debt that we have to

---

[13] Isaiah 53:5.

[14] John 19:28-30.

[15] There is some theological debate about where Jesus's Spirit went during this time and what he did, but none of these various interpretations undermine the truth of his death and our salvation.

[16] Romans 8:1.

[17] Hebrews 4:16.

repay. No one else can hold our sins over us because God no longer accuses us. Though our sins may still have real implications in this life, because of Christ, those implications will not follow us into death and eternity.

We lay down our pride. Seeing the cost of our sin on the cross should cause us to live with humility, especially as we deal with others in their sin, because we needed the sacrifice of Christ just as much as the next person. Observing what it cost God and knowing that we received this free and extravagant gift by faith helps us appreciate and extend grace to others.

We don't have to fear death. Because Jesus went through death on our behalf, we don't have to be afraid of it. Though the reality of death is still scary to us at times, we can look ahead with confidence and say, "O death, where is your victory? O death, where is your sting?"[18] Just as Jesus said to the criminal beside him who trusted in him on the cross, we too can be confident that when we die having trusted Christ, our spirit will immediately go to be with God.[19] We don't have to fear "those who kill the body" or fear that God will forget his promises in the midst of pain, deterioration, or physical suffering.[20] That can give us great courage, boldness, peace, and joy in exceedingly tough situations. We can remember that what Jesus accomplished for us was not trite or hypothetical—he was dead and buried. This gives us so much hope, even as we think of our loved ones who followed Christ but are currently dead and buried.

Jesus Was Raised from the Dead and Ascended to Heaven

As truly as Jesus was dead in the tomb, God's Spirit raised him to life again. As surely as his heart stopped, it started thumping again. His lungs filled with air, and his brain began firing with neurological activity and thoughts. He sat up and stood up and walked out of the tomb. Scripture

---

[18] 1 Corinthians 15:55-58.

[19] Luke 23:39-43.

[20] Matthew 10:28.

assures us that he was not a ghost—his disciples were able to touch his body, see his scars, and watch him eat food.[21] He was also not a figment of a few people's overactive imaginations—he was seen by many people, for extended periods of time, in many different times and places, including one instance where over five hundred eyewitnesses were present.[22] Just as he was fully and totally alive in a resurrected body then, he is still fully alive in his resurrected body now. Scripture tells us that this is only the "firstfruit" and the example of what will happen to every believer.[23]

Though Jesus appeared to many in his resurrected body, his plan was not to stay with his followers on earth. Instead, he had work for them to do and a promise to fulfill. Jesus told his disciples that he would send them a helper—the Holy Spirit—and that this would be better for them as they carried out the kingdom.[24] The Holy Spirit could not come until Jesus departed, and the Spirit would mean not just God's presence among his people as a man but God's presence in every believer. Jesus also gave his followers the Great Commission, the instruction that his disciples were to fulfill and carry out until Christ's return.[25] Jesus ascended to heaven and disappeared into the clouds, and today, he sits at the right hand of God.[26]

Jesus's resurrection and his rule and reign from heaven reframe our experiences now.

We will value our bodies. Though we won't carry disability, disease, or any defect into our resurrected body, we won't become an altogether different version of ourselves. The body we have will be raised from the dead, and we'll have it eternally—God didn't make a mistake with our eye color, skin

---

[21] John 20:20, 27; Luke 24:36-43.

[22] 1 Corinthians 15:3-7.

[23] 1 Corinthians 15:20.

[24] John 16:7.

[25] Matthew 28:18-20.

[26] Acts 1:9.

tone, and so on. Thinking about our bodies in these terms helps us steward them and value them as we wait for them to be raised and glorified.

We will have confidence about our ultimate future, no matter what happens today. As we pray and worship Jesus, we can picture him as he is—a man with a physical body—in the throne room of God. He's not a figment of our imagination or a glowing blob or a floating spirit. He's a physical King and Lord of all, interceding for us at the right hand of God.[27] Resurrection is also a picture of new life and new birth—and when we trust in Christ, our spirits and minds are renewed. Jesus defeated death and the grave to give us new hearts and new desires. We leave the prison cell and tomb of sin and can walk in the freedom of obedience to God. We wait with confidence and hope that Jesus Christ will come again, just as he left. As we face suffering and trials, we trust that having the Spirit in us is really the help we need, and we wait with eager expectation for our final reunion with Christ.

We will have power and purpose in our lives. Jesus's resurrection assures us that Satan and death can't control us or trap us or have power over us anymore, as long as we're united with Christ! This gives us great hope and power in the spiritual battles we face. If we are in Christ, then we have what's called "union with Christ." This means we have God's Spirit dwelling in us, and at any time, we have access to everything we need for life and godliness: God's guidance, wisdom, power over sin, renewed desires, and so on.[28] We ought to consider how to carry out the Great Commission in our own lives, families, communities, and churches. This instruction gives us the overarching mission of our time on earth while we wait for Christ to return.

---

[27] Romans 8:34.

[28] 2 Peter 1:3.

IF WE ARE IN CHRIST, WE HAVE ACCESS TO EVERYTHING WE NEED FOR LIFE & GODLINESS.

We will celebrate diversity in the kingdom of God. We partner with other believers in the Great Commission, all having different gifts and different roles to play, just like all the parts of our body have different jobs but work together under the head (which is Christ). This means we celebrate differences among our Christian friends.

Belonging to Jesus Means Belonging to His People

In all of this, it's important to remember that because of redemption, we're not alone. Not alone in our lives as we face the challenges of the Fall, and not alone in our journey to understand what being a Gospel Mom looks like in our lives. We read in Acts that after Jesus ascended to heaven, he sent the Holy Spirit to live inside believers, and we also see the formation of the first church, which all believers are called to be a part of. Though we might have different interpretations of certain parts of Scripture or even have different thoughts about how to apply certain truths to our lives, those who are truly saved from sin and born again through Christ are adopted into one family—God's family, or the "big C church," which is composed of believers from every tribe, tongue, and nation. We are brothers and sisters, part of the same spiritual bloodline. And we're supposed to care for one another as such—meeting together regularly, praying together, admonishing and encouraging one another, and stirring one another up to love and good works.

Because it's challenging to live as a family with a believer on the other side of the globe or even on the other side of the city, we're called to meet together as local congregations, in local churches. In this context, Christians can know and be accountable to one another more intimately and deeply, counsel one another, face problems and tackle sin together, eat together, pray together, and tangibly help one another in tough seasons. As the New Testament goes on to show us, the church is a huge part of the way redemption plays out in our lives.

We'll talk more about the role of the local church in subsequent chapters, but for now, just keep in mind that it's a critical part of our transformation into Christlikeness as we carry out the Great Commission and live as Gospel Moms.

You Can Do This!

There is a popular Sunday-school-style acronym that might be helpful to remember when you think about this section of the gospel story, and it's spelled like the word *grace*. It reminds us that we have:

God's
Riches
At
Christ's
Expense

Grace undergirds our lives as a Gospel Mom. We know that ultimately, we're not a _____ mom (insert label of choice); we're a woman who was given life abundant—who has the riches of God because of what Christ did for her. Here are some quick questions you can ask when you begin to consider the implications of redemption in your life.

1. How can I look to Christ's example while he was on earth as a model on this topic?

2. Where does Scripture show how Christ has redeemed this topic?

3. How does knowing I am already eternally called "good" before God because of Christ free me to "do good" in this situation through the power of the Holy Spirit?

As Gospel Moms, we have a secure identity and a clear overarching purpose in our lives and in our motherhood. We know we'll face suffering and hardship, that we won't always get it right, and that we'll struggle with shame, fear, and condemnation. But we come back to the cross, and we remember how much God loves us and how much he showed it through Christ. In him, we can walk forward in faith and have love, joy, peace, and hope as we submit to his leading in all things.

CHAPTER 4

CONSUMMATION

O ver the years, our kids have asked a lot of wild questions about heaven: "Will Jesus be so bright that I need sunglasses?" "Will I get to ride a lion?" "Will I be able to eat hot dogs every day?" We wouldn't be caught dead asking these questions out loud in a Bible study, but they aren't that far off from some of the things we've wondered over the years. Many of us have questions when we get to the final part of the gospel framework: Consummation. Like us, you may have wondered, "When exactly is Christ coming?" "What does it look like to rule in God's eternal kingdom?" "Will animals be able to talk there?" Questions like these have certainly engaged theologians for ages and continue to be interesting and fun things to talk and dream about as we consider the final part of God's plan. Yet there are still many things we can know about heaven. While it's true that heaven will be better than anything we can fathom or imagine, God is kind and has given us many concrete things about our eternal home to hold on to in Scripture, which means there is much we can grasp and look forward to.

There are entire books written on this topic that can help you come to a fuller understanding of the consummation of God's plan and the eternal life we will live with him. But for our chapter's purposes today, we'll focus on an overview of what the promised consummation actually is, then spend our time looking at several promises for that day and how they give us freedom and purpose in our lives right now.

The Coming Consummation

Consummation means to finish something or make it perfect.[1] And that's exactly the story God is writing in the Bible. It's the story of how he redeems and restores a sin-wrecked world to a place of perfection in every way. In Redemption, Christ started this process on the cross by defeating Satan and his rule. In Consummation, Christ's rule and reign reach their fullness. It's the "not yet" when we speak about the "already but not yet." Christ has "not yet" come back to judge all people (both the righteous and the wicked), renew the earth, and bring his plan of redemption to completion. But he will.

We don't know the timing of Christ's return, but we do know the main things that will happen:[2] When Christ returns for his people, the dead will be raised and every person will be judged for what they've done.[3] We'll either find our names written in the Lamb's Book of Life or be punished for our wrongdoings on this earth by spending eternity in hell.[4] While believers will face judgment, they don't have to worry or be anxious over this day, knowing Christ bore God's wrath on the cross. After judgment, Satan will be thrown into a lake of burning sulfur to be "tormented day and night forever and ever."[5]

---

[1] Sometimes you'll hear people refer to the four gospel components as Creation / Fall / Redemption / Restoration. As you have probably noted, we're using "Consummation," instead of "Restoration." Here's why: As we discussed in chapter 2, Eden had the potential to be perfect, but it wasn't actually perfect because sin was a possibility (which, as we know, Adam and Eve then engaged in, and we had the Fall). When God completes his plan, sin will no longer be present or a possibility—which means he's not just going to "restore" the earth to its Edenic state; he's going to "consummate" his plan by bringing it to perfect completion. You can use *Restoration* and *Consummation* interchangeably, but *Consummation* seems to better represent what God is going to do someday: unveil something that's far better than what it was before. Definition of consummation is from *Merriam-Webster*, s.v. "consummation," accessed December 13, 2022, https://www.merriam-webster.com/dictionary/consummate.

[2] Matthew 24:36.

[3] John 5:28-29; Romans 2:5-16; Revelation 20:11-3.

[4] Matthew 13:41-43; Daniel 12:2; Revelation 20:15.

[5] Revelation 20:10.

At that time, God will create a new heaven and a new earth, which will be purified from sin.[6] This is the eternal heaven, which we often think of when discussing heavenly things with our family and friends, and it is the destiny of the righteous. Contrary to the way cultural media likes to suggest, heaven won't be "out there," requiring us to take a portal to another land. Instead, God promises to renew this earth by bringing heaven and earth together, like Eden originally was. There, we will have actual bodies, with actual places to go, and actual things to do. Our eternal home will be a world similar to what we know now but free of every evil thing and full of God and his goodness. We'll enjoy God's presence forever, and we'll rule and reign under God over the new creation.

All over the Bible, we read about God fulfilling his promises to bring the world back to its rightful place of perfection and his people to their rightful place of relationship with him. It's foreshadowed in Isaiah, Daniel, and Revelation; promised in the Old Testament narratives; and talked about by Jesus in the Gospels, and we receive exhortation to look forward to it in the epistles. The recovery of perfection is what everything is moving toward, what creation is groaning for, and the culmination of the grand, sweeping story that we're in.

Isaiah 35 gives us a poetic description of what we're looking forward to in in the time of consummation:

> The wilderness and the dry land shall be glad;
>   the desert shall rejoice and blossom like the crocus;
>   it shall blossom abundantly
>   and rejoice with joy and singing.
> The glory of Lebanon shall be given to it,
>   the majesty of Carmel and Sharon.
> They shall see the glory of the LORD,
>   the majesty of our God...

---

[6] Revelation 21:1-3.

OUR ETERNAL HOME WILL BE FULL OF GOD AND HIS GOODNESS.

> Then the eyes of the blind shall be opened,
>   and the ears of the deaf unstopped;
>   then shall the lame man leap like a deer,
>   and the tongue of the mute sing for joy.
> For waters break forth in the wilderness,
>   and streams in the desert.[7]

These poetic lines might feel hard to grasp, but they are meant to paint a picture that points to the overwhelming beauty that awaits us—life with God, glorious, joyful, and perfect. Let's look at some of the promises we know to be true about what we're waiting for.

Always, Only Good

In the chapter on Creation, we told you God only designs good things. It follows that when God restores all of creation for him to dwell with us fully once again, it will only and always be good. The ground won't groan; the weather won't rebel. Animals won't bring violence, and insects won't bite and sting. People won't catch fevers, and our gardens won't grow weeds. In consummation, the effects of the Fall dissipate and disappear. And that includes the ones on humanity. Here are some promises we know from Scripture that await us in our eternal home.

God will dwell with us *(John 14:1-3; Revelation 21:3-5; 22:1)*. The place believers are headed is the place our hearts have always longed to be. This makes all the sense in the world because God is there. While God doesn't have to live anywhere, he has chosen his dwelling place to be heaven.[8] He is now in the present heaven, and when Christ returns and judgment day occurs, he will dwell with us in the new earth.

There will be no sin *(Revelation 21:27)*. In heaven, our sins won't have a hold over us anymore. We will be fully united as people in God, and sin won't be

---

[7] Isaiah 35:1-2, 5-6.

[8] John 14:23.

appealing, exciting, or tempting. Having been united with God through his son and living with the Spirit, sin will be unthinkable, and we won't engage in it.

There will be no pain or hardships *(Revelation 21:4)*. When the new earth is here, the curse of the Fall will be eradicated, and we will no longer feel its effects on our lives. No more "thistles and thorns" or "painful toil"; instead, we will be capable caretakers. We'll have the time, means, and tools necessary to complete our heavenly work, our curse having been removed when Christ became the curse for us.[9]

It won't be boring *(Psalm 16:11)*. Despite the ideas that are often offered to us about eternity, it won't be a place floating forever in the clouds or an eternal worship service. These ideas often make us worry about our experience of eternity, but we don't need to. It won't be boring. This earth and our lives are shadows of God's original design and creation—and he created the sun and the stars, the waterfalls and the oceans. He made adrenaline, music, art, learning, and taste buds. Think of the best experiences you've ever had on this earth. Those are only pale versions of what you will someday enjoy in eternity. This life on earth can truly be incredible—but that's only a tiny taste of what's to come. We can't even begin to comprehend how spectacular and magnificent it will be.

We'll have things to do and places to go *(Revelation 5:13)*. In heaven, we'll be worshipping and glorifying God. But that doesn't mean we'll be hosting sing-alongs and attending church services all day. We saw in the Creation chapter that in Eden, Adam and Eve were given the cultural mandate to rule over the earth and develop arts, culture, and crafts. We continue that work today, but it's riddled with difficulty due to the curse. In heaven, we'll keep expanding on the cultural mandate, but we'll be uninhibited by sin or the curse. Like he did for Adam and Eve, God will delegate certain roles and

---

[9] Galatians 3:13.

responsibilities over creation to us. We'll build and create, gain skills and knowledge, and have resources and opportunities that never end.

Our deepest longings for family and friendships will be met *(Mark 10:29-30)*. As believers, we all have different relationships with our earthly families. Some have loving families, and others have difficult or even abusive families, but in heaven, we will be one big harmonious family. And while there won't be marriage in an earthly sense, there will be one perfect union between Christ and his bride—that's us![10] As one family, we'll experience renewed and perfected relationships in ways we can't even fathom here below.

We'll eat and drink—we'll feast *(Isaiah 25:6; Luke 22:29-30)!* Multiple places in Scripture mention eating in the eternal heaven. Think of the best meal you've ever had in your life. Someday in heaven, you will smile at that innocent idea of what good food tasted like as you eat the best food you've ever had. Our taste buds, affected today by the curse, will explode with a new understanding of flavor. We won't overeat or undereat in heaven, which means no more stomachaches or feeling weak or tired.

We will spend time with Jesus, ruling and reigning with him *(John 14:3; Isaiah 25:6; Luke 12:37)*. Have you ever imagined what it would be like to be a disciple of Jesus in the New Testament, walking and talking with him every day? Someday, you'll no longer have to imagine it—it will be your reality. Scripture promises we will be with our Savior when we die. And the incredible thing is that Jesus will not just spend time with us, but he will spend time serving us. What humility! What kindness!

Pretty incredible, right? In the midst of all of this, it's important for us to realize that the very best thing we'll have in heaven is being fully in the presence of God for eternity, totally unencumbered by any hint of guilt or shame.

---

[10] Matthew 22:30.

How Our Promised Future Matters Right Now

It's easy to think that all these future realities are just for, well, the future. But the Bible tells us over and over that those promises are for our good even now. That's why when people talk about consummation, they can mean a couple of different things. *Sometimes*, people are specifically referencing the moment in time when Christ returns and the church is united with him forever, which we talked about earlier in the chapter. But other times, when people are talking about consummation, they are also *generally* referring to the hope of the eternal inheritance we have in heaven. It's the hope that reminds us that this life isn't the end of our story and we won't always live with the effects of sin and the brokenness of the Fall. And that leads us to the natural next question we have as Gospel Moms: *How can these insights about heaven change my thinking here and now? How can they help me press on toward heaven and seek the things above?* There are thousands of ways, but here are a few ways these truths about heaven encourage us and apply to our lives today.

Our bodies matter, and we should care for them. Because our bodies will be resurrected at the coming of Christ, we know that God cares about them and that we should too. This doesn't mean we need to work out all the time, eat perfectly, or spend thousands of dollars on skincare products. No matter what we do, our outer selves are still "wasting away" and will eventually age and meet physical death. But it does mean that we should acknowledge their limits and care for them accordingly. All of us have different levels of ability, so this will look different for each individual, but where we're able, we can look to maintain a level of fitness, seek the right amount of sleep, eat nourishing foods, drink enough water, and so on. Our bodies are not just containers for our souls but will one day be transformed for eternity. As Gospel Moms, we honor God's design by caring for our bodies now to the best of our ability so we can do his work on the earth while also knowing one day God will renew them.

It gives us a new perspective on suffering. The promise of complete restoration means God will also renew our experiences and circumstances. If Redemption reveals the purpose in our suffering, Consummation gives us hope in it. Paul says that the sufferings of this present time are not worth comparing to the glory that will one day be revealed.[11] Knowing that someday a child will be healed, a parent will no longer suffer from a disease, our own disability will be gone, or we will see our loved one who has passed away—this gives us hope in the midst of sorrow.

It gives us hope in the midst of earthly chaos. Watch the first ten minutes of the evening news, and you'll see the horrific injustices of the world. Our hearts ache when we hear of violence against women or children, families caught up as innocent casualties of war, or the mistreatment and abuse of a child. But we know God will make all things right, judge the wicked, and exact vengeance on those who have oppressed others and made them suffer. Satan is on a leash—he will be stopped. His reign and rule won't last forever.[12] As Gospel Moms, it's still hard to face these realities, but we can do justice as we are able and trust that full justice is coming. It will be swift and true.

It gives meaning to our work and lives. We know from the Great Commission that making disciples is our primary work, and as Gospel Moms, this includes sharing the gospel with our children and teaching them the ways of God. But it also means we want to share the good news of Jesus beyond the four walls of our homes and find ways to be missionaries with other people as witnesses of God's goodness to the world. This should change how we spend our time and money, how we prioritize relationships, and how we view others. Scripture ends with a picture of every tribe, nation, and tongue all gathered for a feast in the new heavens and the new earth.[13] It's an

---

[11] Romans 8:18.

[12] Revelation 20:10.

[13] Revelation 7; 19.

inspiring glimpse of what heaven will be like, and it's also what we can work toward right now. We should be intentional with the work God has given us here to do and be wise stewards of the short time we have on this earth.

We can have contagious joy in all things. As humans, it's a fairly universal trait that when we find out about something amazing—a song, a drink, or a show—we want to tell everybody about it. That's because it's how we are designed—to overflow with excitement when we encounter a good thing and to want to share it with others. We can encourage our fellow believers in the promises of Christ that we've experienced. Knowing the "inside scoop" should compel us to share the gospel message with everyone around us.

It gives the church meaning and importance. The work God has given us isn't just for the individual; it's also for his church collectively. Knowing there will only be one marriage and one family in heaven, we model that today by seeing other believers as our family in Christ. We should invest deeply in our church family now, knowing it's a small picture of what we will experience for eternity.

It gives us a firm hope to cling to as we live our lives now. The hope of heaven is helpful in our sufferings, and it's also encouraging in the mundane moments—when we're tired of doing the dishes yet again, feeling worn down by yet another bill showing up in the mail, or feeling frustrated by our own anger or impatience with our children. We have an inheritance that will never perish, fade, or spoil, and someday the curse will be broken and we'll be set free from all our sinful habits and the groaning of life on this earth.[14]

It reminds us that we don't have to "do" everything in this life. Instead of feeling like we have to accomplish every dream or goal as soon as possible, we know that the Lord has numbered our days and we have an eternity of joy to look forward to. This mindset makes us willing to lose our lives because they aren't our "one shot." We can receive from the Lord all he has

---

[14] 1 Peter 1:4.

for us and know that it is just for a short time, as our best life isn't behind us, and it isn't now—it's yet to be after this life is over.

We don't fear death. And as believers, we are promised if we trust in Christ, we will have eternal life with God forever.[15] Our sure and certain future means we don't have to fear death. Whether we live or die, no one can give us something better than what we already have, and no one can take away anything that we truly need. We can trust God with the timeline of our earthly life, knowing when we die, it means we finally get to be with our precious Savior.

Sister, if you have repented and put your faith in Jesus and you're walking with him by faith, then you don't have to fear this day; your eternity is secure.[16] But if you're unsure or thinking you want more time to make a decision, we beg you—don't wait. "Yet you do not know what tomorrow will bring. What is your life? For you are a mist that appears for a little time and then vanishes."[17] You don't know what tomorrow holds or whether you will live or die. If you trust in Christ, you don't have to worry. You know for certain that heaven is your final destination and have hope today that changes everything.[18] Someday, your knee will bow to Christ—let it be now, and not when it's too late.

You Can Do This!

You might find that some days on this earth, you feel a bit restless, like you're not quite settled or haven't fully come into your own yet. While that

---

[15] John 3:16; 2 Corinthians 4:17; John 17:3.

[16] John 6:47.

[17] James 4:14.

[18] John 20:31.

might bother you, it's actually fairly healthy. Scripture tells us that we are aliens and sojourners on this earth; we should expect to feel out of place. It's like what Paul writes in Romans about how our souls "groan inwardly as we wait eagerly" for the new creation.[19] Feeling unsettled in this way is a holy discontentment—a longing to go to your true home in heaven while also knowing you have work to do here on earth. As Christians, our lives often feel like continual paradoxes—we hold a lot of opposite things in tension all the time. And part of that is living in this space between Christ's death and resurrection and his coming earthly reign.

When we strive to apply the truths of consummation to our own lives as Gospel Moms, we can ask questions like the following:

1. How does the assurance of future hope in eternity change my perspective and give me a purpose and a mission today?

2. How can I trust that God is working for my greatest good in this situation, knowing he is sovereign and I am part of the greater story he is writing?

3. Someday Christ will perfectly administer all justice and make all things right. How can that give me comfort today?

We don't know when Christ will return. But we do know he's going to come like a thief in the night, and as Gospel Moms, we want to be ready.[20] This is the hope we cling to as we drive our minivans to soccer practice, pick up pizza for a birthday party, clean throw up from the carpet in the middle of the night, hook up a G-tube for another feeding, or visit the gravestone of

---

[19] Romans 8:23.

[20] 1 Thessalonians 5:2-4.

the child we only held for a few hours. In all of this, we can look to the hope of heaven. Until his return, we watch, we wait, we remain faithful to what God has in front of us—hoping not in what we can see but in the unseen realm that is our final destination.

PART 2

THE PRACTICES

SPIRITUAL DISCIPLINES
AND HABITS

Okay, deep breath. After all those chapters on the four parts of the gospel, you might be feeling like you're in information overload and wondering how you'll sort it out to understand what it looks like to glorify God in your daily decisions and circumstances. Hold tight, because we're on the road to get there. We know even if you've been a believer for a long time, thinking through the gospel story and its implications can feel overwhelming. We've given you the CliffsNotes version, and with practice and repetition, you'll know it more deeply and get the hang of viewing daily situations of motherhood through a gospel lens. We promise!

But we're guessing you're wondering this: In the midst of school pickup, doctor's appointments, soccer practice, and your husband's travel schedule—seriously, *how* do you practice getting the framework of the gospel under your skin? How do you practically learn it and make it a part of your life, as natural as pouring a cup of coffee or sweeping a crying child into your arms?

Well, like anything else you want to learn, you have to make intentional choices and invest time.

We know that's not the fun answer or how most of us hope to learn—we

TO LEARN, YOU HAVE TO MAKE INTENTIONAL CHOICES AND INVEST TIME.

want the instant-download version. But we aren't robots. We're people. And God has created us to learn through time, thought, intention, and repetition.

Think of it like this: You've been inspired to learn to bake homemade sourdough bread. The online influencers and your friend up the road make it look achievable, and who wouldn't love a freshly baked loaf of bread on their table every night? So you set out to learn. First, you read recipes and watch others bake bread. Then you gain a base knowledge of how bread making works. You purchase the right tools, then follow the recipe. Maybe you even have a chance to work alongside a skilled bread baker and ask questions. Eventually, after dozens of loaves and lots of trial and error, you learn a couple of recipes by heart. If you keep at it weekly or even daily, it will eventually become a natural action to whip together a fresh loaf. It's when you can bake by heart and teach it to others that you actually *know* it—and this is the kind of gospel knowledge we hope you'll achieve over time.

So if the most important part of growing as a Gospel Mom is knowing Christ and the truth of the gospel, we're going to have to establish a means for that growth to occur. Our faith and salvation aren't earned by what we do, but regular spiritual disciplines and habits (like Bible study, prayer, corporate worship, and patterns of rest) create conditions that make us ripe for growth in Christian maturity. By the Spirit's power, they're what allow us to go from *wanting* to spend more time with the Lord and think through a gospel lens to actually *being able* to do it. Every small yet hopeful beginning needs consistent care and investment over a long period of time if it's going to mature into something strong.

These two topics—spiritual disciplines and habits—are what we'll explore in part 2 of this book. They're how we create heart conditions optimal for spiritual health, for the sake of serving in God's kingdom and getting the glory of the gospel story under our skin.

Spiritual Disciplines: Our Support Stake

If we are like a plant, spiritual disciplines are like the stake we grow on. Both of us enjoy having live plants in our homes and outdoor gardens, and our beloved plants need various things for growth. Many of them benefit from stakes or a trellis to support them as they lean toward the light, keeping them upright so they can freely mature and produce flowers. Between the Iowa wind and the dull winter sun, unsupported plants have the tendency to sag and bend toward the ground, becoming stunted and unhealthy. This is much like our faith. As true followers of Christ, the Spirit will continue his work in our hearts, but without the stake or trellis of regular spiritual disciplines, our growth might stagnate. We might lose focus on the light of Christ and start to bend toward other things. Spiritual disciplines are regular practices that help us lean toward the light, stay committed to Christ, and create ripe conditions for maturity and good fruit. They help us stay tethered to God and his Word through every season.

As we explored in part 1, God's Word is where we go to learn and understand God's design and plan for his people. Not just in general but also in our individual lives and situations. We can only be Gospel Moms insofar as we walk by the Spirit and know how the Word of God applies to our lives. Since Scripture is without error, never faltering or changing, it's the focus of our disciplines as we seek to worship God and understand his will for our lives.

Spiritual Habits: The Regular Care

But a stake isn't the only thing a plant needs for optimal growth. As we've cared for the plants in our own homes, we've discovered that each plant has common yet unique needs for flourishing. They all need some level of light, water, and nutrition—but when and how much? That's a whole different question! We've had to learn each plant's unique needs—how frequently it needs water, how much sun or shade it can handle during each season of the year, and when and how much it needs to be fertilized or pruned. In the same way that plants need regular care, we need regular rhythms of soul care to help us thrive and flourish. Spiritual habits help us notice our own needs, and then prune, pull weeds, and cultivate the environment so we may be healthy in every season.

Just like we don't want our plants to barely limp along for months because we won't take time to trim off their dead leaves, we don't want our kingdom impact and motherhood to suffer because we've ignored our God-given needs. Many of these needs and habits are inferred as we observe how God created humankind (like noticing that our bodies do best with good nutrition and sleep) or they are explicitly modeled or commanded in Scripture (like the command to rest—as illustrated in the practice of Sabbath). Even though it's easy to come up with a list of regular things we should do for optimal spiritual, physical, and mental health, it's difficult to know how to put those things into practice. Like plant care, it's an art of observation and wisdom—noticing that when the leaves are drooping, extra watering might be needed, or when the leaves are dull, a good wiping would be nice to remove the layer of dust. We don't necessarily need a regimented, uninterrupted routine of perfect spiritual habits, but we need an awareness of these habits so that we can tend to them as the Lord leads us in each season.

So back to the question from the start of this section: *How do we actually become proficient in knowing the gospel in the midst of our busy lives as moms?* We make the choice to prioritize it, knowing that the dividends of the investment in spiritual disciplines and habits will pay off in our ability to lead faithful, flourishing lives for God's glory. We're like plants, remember? Let's get our trellis up and find the sun.

CHAPTER 5

SPIRITUAL DISCIPLINES

Sometimes it feels impossible to be both a growing Christian *and* a mom. We know this firsthand. You wake up early to read the Bible? They wake up early. You stay up late for some quiet meditation on the Word? They come home at curfew and finally want to talk. You sneak away to a coffee shop for a couple of hours to read the Word and journal? Your husband texts before your latte even cools down enough to drink to let you know that someone just vomited (so if you can cut it just a little short and come help, that would be awesome).

We remember being young mothers and asking, "Are the little years the lost years of spiritual growth?" And honestly, every stage of parenting we've entered has welcomed us with a whole new reason why this season isn't a good time for spiritual growth. While all the obstacles in every stage are very real, they aren't as high or as insurmountable as they feel. Even if reading the word *disciplines* makes you feel fatigued, annoyed, pressured, or overwhelmed, we want to encourage you to take heart and stick with us. The point of this section, and of examining the ways we can stake our lives to the Word of God, isn't to add another thing to the to-do list. It's not to make gospel motherhood harder—but easier. Lighter. More full, fruitful, and free. If we are like plants and spiritual disciplines are our trellis, we need their support to grow strong! This is exactly what Jesus means when he says, "Take my yoke upon you, and learn from me, for I am gentle and lowly in heart, and you will find rest for your souls. For my yoke is easy, and my burden is light."[1] As we know Christ through his Word and walk with him, we have the resources we need to find rest for our souls.

What mom doesn't want that?

As we talk about the spiritual disciplines that can help shape our understanding of God—so that you can walk with and glorify him as a Gospel Mom—we hope you get excited about the support they can provide, not discouraged about one more good thing that has been added to your to-do list.

Spiritual Disciplines Stake Us to the Word of God

One of the issues with staking our lives to the wisdom of the age (the tips of our favorite influencers, our best friend's advice, or our mom subculture guru) is that this "wisdom" is ever-changing. Give it a few weeks, months, or years, and the latest child-development research will report something different, the influencer will find a never-before-heard-of method you need to adopt, your friend will have a bad experience and change her tune, or the guru will add more impossible rules. If we try to chew on and grow from their words, they'll eventually lose taste or become bitter. We'll have to rip out the thing that was holding up some part of our lives and put in a new stake every time they retract a statement or change their guidance.

It's not that there is no wisdom to be had out there—some sleep-training expert might be able to actually help our child nap better, or a mom friend's insight on a new book series might help us avoid content we didn't want our kids to read. But there is a difference between listening to and discerning another person's words and staking our lives on them. Remember, Gospel Moms aren't loyal to a mom lifestyle or method or friend group; they're loyal to the Word of Life himself. We build our lives on the Bible as the authoritative basis for truth, thinking, and decision-making. We don't always understand God's Word as clearly or as easily as we'd like to, but it is without

---

[1] Matthew 11:29-30.

error. It reveals who God is and his plan for humankind. His words are sweet and eternal, trustworthy and true. Scripture has the power to transform our hearts and illuminate our thinking, helping us discern God's will.

The stake of spiritual disciplines is meant to tether us to Scripture the way a vine is tethered to a trellis. Jesus said we can't live on bread alone, but on "every word that comes from the mouth of God."[2] Jesus himself is the living Word and the bread of life—knowing him intimately and deeply is what nourishes our hearts and gives us deep peace. When believers practice Communion—the breaking of bread and drinking of juice or wine—we show that we believe a different kind of food, a spiritual food, sustains us and causes us to grow in the Lord.[3]

We can't live by something we don't know or haven't taken care to understand. But with each return to the pages of Scripture, the roots of our understanding strengthen and drive deeper. While there are a myriad of ways to ingest the Word of God, and there aren't "rules" around how to do it, there are some tried-and-true practices that can help us as we abide in Christ. We're going to walk through a few of them in this chapter. Perhaps you already do many or all of these things, so if this is familiar territory, don't feel like you have to add more. We find that even though we've walked with Christ for a long time, we still need reminders to prioritize these things as we evaluate our disciplines in each season.

Read the Bible Regularly, in Different Ways

Have you ever heard the words *plow* and *trowel*? These agricultural terms are sometimes used to describe different ways of engaging with the Bible. The word *trowel* is meant to help us envision digging a shovel down deep into one specific spot—think of it as mining or seeking to obtain every precious thing in each area of Scripture. (It's what we'll talk about in the next

---

[2] Matthew 4:4.

[3] John 6:54.

KNOWING JESUS INTIMATELY & DEEPLY IS WHAT GIVES US DEEP PEACE.

section.) But the word *plow* should bring to mind a picture of a farm implement covering a large swath of land. Its goal isn't to stay in one place but to go corner to corner across the field, similar to reading a book of the Bible or the entire Bible (cover to cover!) to get an overview of the story of redemption. When we take time to read the Word (or listen to it), whether it's a few chapters, a whole book, or a larger section of Scripture, that's exactly what we're doing—plowing through.

The plowing that happens in reading and the troweling that happens in Bible study both prepare our spiritual soil. Simply reading the Word, or having it read to you, works. Like any good story, repetition gets it into our bones, helping us with comprehension and recall. Few of us set out to memorize the fairy tales or favorite picture books we read as a child, and yet going through those pages over and over was enough to sink the story down deep into our memory banks until it became a part of us in some way. This is all the more true for the living and active Word of God. To read the Word more often in a "plow" method, you might consider:

- adopting an annual Bible reading plan

- listening to the Bible daily or weekly in your morning routine or on a walk

- reading the Bible out loud to your kids or during a family devotional

- having a regular time of day or days of the week when you sit down and read large sections of Scripture, be it a few chapters or even a whole book of the Bible

- reading one book of the Bible over and over again to build comprehension of the text

- being part of a church that emphasizes the reading of God's Word in corporate worship

Another way to think about this is to "eat regular meals." Most of us eat at least three times a day because we realize that without food, we're weak and tired (and cranky). Well, the same is true of our hearts apart from the strengthening of God's Word. We have unprecedented access to the Bible, and yet many of us go days, weeks, or even years without spending meaningful time consuming it. If you wouldn't go days (or hours) without food, why would you go a long time between spiritual meals? It doesn't have to be duty or drudgery—but consider what it would look like to immerse yourself in the Word so that you can be an even better student when it's time to trowel.

Study the Bible

As mentioned in the previous section, *troweling* is the process of digging deep into Scripture so we can understand, interpret, and apply God's Word to our lives. Deep study and learning of a particular topic equip us with the depth of information we need to problem-solve in real-world situations. Studying Scripture is what helps us take the things we read in the Bible and give them meaning and context (even the most difficult parts, like those genealogies, gory battles, or confusing laws). This might seem daunting at first—like an overwhelming and impossible task—but you will be so glad that you invested your time in this process. Even the most seasoned Christian gets fatigued by Bible study sometimes and needs a little reinvigoration, so if you're already familiar with this, we hope it's a helpful reminder or motivation for how you might bring other moms alongside you in the process!

If you're not sure where to jump in, here are a few ideas:

- Join a Bible study at your local church or in your community.
- Work through a guided Bible study book on your own or with a group of friends (maybe even one with a corresponding video or podcast option for further commentary).
- Listen to, watch, or audit a free seminary course that digs deeper into a part of Scripture or book of the Bible.

- Follow along closely with your pastor's sermon series as it covers a book of the Bible by doing your own reading, study, and note-taking.

- Journal through a book of the Bible, pausing to reflect, obtain clarification about confusing passages, and write about things that stand out to you.

Perhaps our favorite method of study (and the one that has been the most accessible and helped us discover the most truth for ourselves) is the inductive method. We certainly didn't invent inductive study—it's a widely known method of studying Scripture. If you want to try inductive Bible study, we have a free guide at the end of this book (in appendix E) to give you all the details. It's a helpful step-by-step guide that doesn't require more than your Bible, a pen, and a heart ready to learn.

If reading Scripture is kind of like opening a big map so you can get the lay of the land, studying it is a bit like understanding the map's details so you can see how each part fits into the big picture. In fact, applying the gospel in motherhood (as we laid out in part 1 with CFRC) gets clearer with a deep understanding of God's Word. As you find clarity, you grow in confidence, learning to apply the gospel rightly in whatever situation you're facing in motherhood.

Spend Time Thinking About What the Bible Says

Have you ever watched a cooking show where the chef takes the first bite of the dish they've been working on for the last hour and really savors it? After they describe the flavor profile, the texture, and the temperature (with language you wouldn't have thought to apply to food), you feel like you almost tasted that bite yourself. Most moms wolf down meals because we're running from one activity to the next. Or maybe we're the last one to sit down, or the food is cold anyway, so we might be out of the habit of really chewing our food—let alone savoring it. But savoring food is an incredible practice to help us appreciate and understand the complexity and depth of what we're eating before we swallow it. Even from a scientific standpoint, chewing our food sufficiently makes it easier for the stomach to digest.

If we take this analogy and apply it to the Word of God, we become the taste tester at the table of our Lord, experiencing our faith in ways that light up our spiritual palate. Some people refer to this practice as Scripture meditation. In this, we can be like the psalmist and the tree planted beside streams of living water as we "meditate [on the Scriptures] day and night."[4] This type of meditation isn't about relaxation, clearing your mind of all thoughts, focusing on certain breathing techniques or feelings in the body, or even repeating the same thing over and over again. It's about ruminating, mulling over, and reflecting on a passage of Scripture over a period of time.

Scripture meditation doesn't have to be something you set aside specific time for each day (although you could!), but it should be something you do throughout the day as you remember God and his words. Here are some ideas to get started:

- Put a note card or Post-it note of a verse you want to remember and place it in a noticeable location so you can read and think of it often (maybe while you're doing a mundane task like washing dishes or driving to work).

- See if you can find the verse you want to ponder as a song online (a surprising number of these exist), and listen to it often. Or put the verse to your own tune or beat in your head so it becomes easy to remember.

- Journal or pray about that verse (more to come on prayer below), breaking it down into smaller words or phrases so you can really consider the meaning.

---

[4] Psalm 1:2.

- Set the verse as your smartphone lock screen, and take a second to say it to yourself before you open your phone.

When we store God's Word in our hearts by committing it to memory, we're able to bring it to mind in any part of our lives as we seek to better understand God's meaning in it and for us.

Pray

The topic of prayer is expansive. And rightly so—talking to God is a fundamental privilege of his people. It's not only a spiritual discipline that we do as part of our growth in God's Word, but it's also an essential part of being a Gospel Mom who communes with God and abides in Christ. Prayer is talking with God as we pour out our hearts to him and think deeply about what he's said to us in his Word. There are many types of and components to prayer, but here are some things to note:

Prayers can come in many forms. You can pray by talking out loud, thinking in your head, writing prayers down, singing (including "praying" a worship song or hymn), listening to or agreeing with the prayers of others, or reading God's Word with a heart to use those verses as your own prayer. You can pray standing or sitting down or while walking or even while you're in bed. Because God is everywhere and has full knowledge of what's in your mind and heart, all you have to do is direct your thoughts to him, and you can engage in prayer.

Prayers don't have to be a certain style or length. Even though in many cases, believers start by addressing God the Father in the name of Jesus and closing with a phrase like "amen" (which essentially expresses that we entrust all to the Lord), that's not the only model for prayer. Prayers can be a word or a short phrase, long and drawn out, done with others, done in public, or done in private.

Prayers come from a place of reverence and humility. It's okay to approach the throne of grace with joy and confidence through Christ. We can have warm, loving, and even lighthearted conversations with God (jumping and leaping and praising God or making a joyful noise to the Lord are just a few descriptions given of people who did this in the Bible), but we do want to remember that God is the sovereign Lord of the universe, that he's holy and righteous. We don't approach him like he's a disposable friend or a genie in a bottle.

Prayers should be rooted in the things God has already said about himself in the Bible. Scripture verses make a great basis for prayer as we add our own thoughts, questions, and concerns. This helps us make sure we're asking for things that are in accordance with God's will.

As mentioned above, prayer can take many forms, but a common tool to help us remember aspects of prayer we might want to cover is the mnemonic device commonly referred to as ACTS:

A: Adoration is praising God for who he is and what he's done. This is a great way to start our prayer, and it can be the whole prayer we pray!

C: Confession is a chance to share and be transparent about our hearts with God, including areas where we've sinned, we're fearful, or we're struggling.

T: Thanksgiving is something God commands us to do in Scripture, and it's a chance to remember that God is the giver of all things and has already given us so much grace.

S: Supplication is a big word that just means asking God for what we need or desire. There's a reason why supplication is at the end of this particular model for prayer—because going through the other parts first helps shape our asking in ways that are more likely to fall in line with God's revealed will and character.

This isn't the only way to pray—for instance, in forms of prayer like lament, someone might spend almost the entire prayer in confession and supplication. The ACTS approach is just one example to practice.

Why should a Gospel Mom pray?

We know you have enough on your plate already (and you may feel talked out), but we promise that prayer won't add burdens—it will lift them. When you pray, God will change your heart to further align your thoughts and motives with his Word. God will give you perspective and remind you of the part you play in the redemption storyline—to serve him and love others. As you pray, you'll also become more and more aware of God's presence and care. The more you talk with him, the more you'll spot his hand in your life. Prayer is an active display of humility as you go to God for wisdom and clarity in your questions, concerns, and hard decisions. It's like saying, "I don't have all the answers, but I trust the one who does." Also, moms are great at practically loving those in their care, but did you know that prayer is one of the very best ways you can care for others, especially in situations that are beyond what your hands and heart can handle? Finally, when you pray, you never know how God is going to use it. Maybe it was your prayers that God worked in and through as a means of healing or change or even salvation. When you pray, you can be an example to your husband, your children, and your community, where peace and hope are truly found.

As Gospel Moms, we pray to God and trust that through his Spirit, his Word, our circumstances, and the wise guidance of God's people, we'll be guided to walk more and more in his ways.

Go to Church

In all of this, it's crucial to remember that we weren't meant to read, study, or apply God's Word or live gospel motherhood in a silo. Instead of eating all our spiritual meals at home alone, we're invited to the table with God's people to feast and fellowship together. We can do this first and foremost as

"I DON'T HAVE ALL THE ANSWERS, BUT I TRUST THE ONE WHO DOES."

part of a local church—a body of believers who come together on a regular basis in corporate worship to read, study, meditate on, and pray the Word as a group. We can also do this in smaller groups of believers, where we can study more deeply and pray for one another more vulnerably. Whether with a mentor or a few close-believing friends, we can also remind one another of the gospel, giving clarity, wisdom, or counsel.

When we sing together, pray together, open the Bible together, remind one another of God's promises, take Communion, and live out our lives side by side, we participate in a practice that strengthens not only our faith but the faith of the whole church.

Go Further

Many words have been written covering practices and habits that help us grow in our understanding and application of the gospel. The ones laid out here are not the only options! You can do more research on your own and look into habits like fasting (abstaining from food or a habit for a period of time for the sake of more fully focusing your attention on Christ), silence and solitude (spending time in quiet by yourself to pray and reflect in a more intentional way, making space to hear from God), and acts of giving or service (intentionally focusing on helping others in a regular way to remind you of your greater purpose in God's kingdom).

In the next chapter, we're going to dive into other rhythms and practices that are important to the life of a Gospel Mom and are not always characterized as spiritual disciplines.

CHAPTER 6

SPIRITUAL HABITS

There's a joke we have at Risen Motherhood that a mom's season changes—at minimum—every three months. The moment you feel like things are under control and you've discovered a good rhythm for your life and family, everything collapses faster than a Jenga tower. When we were new mothers, we found this at best a bit irksome—and at worst, infuriating. As we tried to keep up with food trends, school choice variables, medical needs, or seasonal schedules, our hearts were anxious and our worries in overdrive, and we seemed to consistently live on the edge of our limits. We found ourselves asking, *Is this really the abundant life we read about in Scripture?*

In the last chapter, we focused mainly on rooting ourselves in the Word of God through spiritual disciplines. We talked about reading the Word, studying the Word, meditating on the Word, praying the Word, and coming together around the Word. That's a lot of Word! But we shouldn't stop there. We want our faith to move from the head to the heart. We want to truly apprentice under Jesus. To do that, we must take what we learn in Scripture and apply it to our daily lives through our habits, rhythms, and practices. These habits of spiritual formation help us live in a way where we are consistently growing and maturing in our faith and giving God glory in all that we do.

Peter writes, "For this very reason, make every effort to supplement your faith with virtue, and virtue with knowledge, and knowledge with self-control, and self-control with steadfastness, and steadfastness with godliness, and godliness with brotherly affection, and brotherly affection with love. For if these qualities are yours and are increasing, they keep you from being ineffective or unfruitful in the knowledge of our Lord Jesus Christ."[1] As Gospel Moms, this is what we want! To be "effective" and "fruitful" in our faith. But to do that, we must build our lives in ways that cultivate an inner transformation toward Christlikeness. Sticking with the plant analogy from the introduction of this section, this is like tending to the needs of the plant through consistent care like watering, light placement, and pruning.

What we've noticed about the plants in our own homes is that every plant is unique in the exact kind of care they need. Some need water every week, and others can go a month between waterings. Some plants like full, bright sun on their leaves every day of the week, and others like to stick to the shadows. Some need pruning every few months, and others need it once a year. Anytime we've moved a plant in a significant way, we've found they always needed a season of extra nurturing to recover from the shock of the changing environment. As Laura's mom says, "Caring for plants is an art! You just have to discover what helps them thrive."

If the spiritual disciplines we discussed in the last chapter are the stake, the spiritual habits we'll explore in this chapter are the pruning, weeding, and soil cultivation that help the plant bud, flower, and produce fruit all year long. All of us will come to these practices in different ways depending on our personalities, life circumstances, abilities, and more, but we'll talk about how to discover that in the next chapter. For now, we're going to work through some of the patterns and practices we find in Scripture (and see in wise people's lives) that allow God's people to lead a flourishing life—the abundant life that Scripture talks about. Of course, this isn't an exhaustive

---

[1] 2 Peter 1:5-8.

list; there are many practices other than what we've covered here. We've chosen to only highlight a handful that we've seen come up again and again in our motherhood, but there are many other habits that are relevant to and helpful for the care we need as moms.

If you're feeling like a plant that just made a major move, perhaps reengaging in some of the practices below will help bring you new life.

Habit of Curation

We've all been there. That zombie feeling when you've binge-watched too much TV and feel out of sorts with yourself. Or you've had your phone in your hand too much for a day, and you feel guilty about only giving your children half your attention. Or perhaps you just read a book that wasn't as "closed-door romance" as you thought, and you feel distressed over not skipping those pages or even putting down the book entirely. As Christians, there's a reason we feel unsettled or regretful after we consume something we know we shouldn't have—whether that's the amount of content or the content itself. Either way, the reason it produces a response in us is that our media habits have profound effects on us. The books we read, the podcasts and music we listen to, the TV we watch, the social media we consume—all of it is formative to our souls. As the old saying goes, "What goes in must come out." If we're feeling anxious, tired, angry, or overwhelmed, a good thing to evaluate is our media consumption.

To grow as Gospel Moms, we want to choose a quantity and quality of media that help us love God more, not less. If we have a toxic media diet, whether that means excessive social media consumption, heavy partisan news sources, or raunchy podcasts, it's going to poison our hearts and shift our love toward sin instead of righteousness. Scripture tells us that what is in our hearts is what comes out in our day-to-day lives: "The good person out of the good treasure of his heart produces good, and the evil person out of his evil treasure produces evil, for out of the abundance of the heart his mouth speaks."[2] But media can also be used to stir our emotions toward Christ. Remember, God is the originator of story, art, and beauty, and through using wisdom, we can find books, movies, and podcasts that stir our emotions toward worship. So we have to consistently ask, *Is media helping or hurting my love for Christ?* Here are a few questions for beginning the habit of curation:

- Does this media help me love God more?

- Does this media treat humans with dignity and respect as image bearers of God (even when it displays the complexity of human experience and emotion)?

- Does this media shape my emotions in a way that makes it so I can't sleep or function regularly in daily life?

- Can I give this media up entirely and still find happiness and joy in life and, ultimately, in Christ?

- Am I using this media as an unhealthy distraction or a way to check out from my real-life responsibilities?

As Gospel Moms, what are we giving our time and attention to? Let's curate our media habits in a way that shapes our love and therefore our worship toward the only one worthy of it: Jesus Christ.

Habit of Friendship

One of the most frequent things we hear from mothers is that they feel all alone in their motherhood journey. Perhaps it's after their first child is born, and suddenly they're home all day with no adults to speak to. Or it's in the teen years, and they're working all day and running around at night with no time for true friendships of their own. Or maybe it's in a season of deep suffering, and their world feels small, with no one who they feel has walked

---

[2] Luke 6:45.

WHAT ARE WE GIVING OUR TIME & ATTENTION TO?

the same path. What we're lacking is friendship. In our modern age, we've become more used to surface-level friends and online acquaintances, and sometimes we can even catch ourselves believing that an online influencer can fill the place of a true friend. But God designed us for more than superficial relationships. He made us with a deep (and good) desire for belonging.

God tells us he "sets the lonely in families" [3]—first and foremost through Christ as we become a part of his church, but he also leads us to friends in various seasons of life, so we may walk with and care for one another. But sometimes that doesn't look like what we expected (or even hoped for). It might mean a more seasoned mom comes alongside us to teach us about the work of the home. It might mean a single friend with a more flexible schedule comes over after the kids are in bed. It might mean grabbing lunch with a co-worker once a week. And more than likely, it means there will be a handful of different friends because no one person can meet all your needs. If we do have a season where we are truly lonely or isolated, we can ask God to bring us a friend. But even if the Lord doesn't give us the friend we hoped for in our ideal timing, we can know that ultimately, we have true friendship and belonging in Christ. Here are some ways to invest in the habit of friendship:

- Work on being the friend you would want to have.
- Keep right expectations for what a friendship can do and be.
- Prioritize time with friends as regularly as you can.
- Be a good question-asker, and be an even better listener.
- Be willing to take risks—be vulnerable in order to receive vulnerability back.
- Don't expect deep friendships to occur overnight. Give them time and care.

---

[3] Psalm 68:6 NIV.

- Celebrate your friends' joys, and share in their sorrows.

- Be selfless. Consider others more important than yourself in the way you speak, listen, and act.

Habit of Nature

As moms, it can be easy to feel like our world consists of our home, our phone screens, and maybe our work and our children's schools. If we're not intentional, weeks may go by where we might not actually get out into nature aside from a quick walk from the car to the next place we're going! But going outdoors reminds us of our place in the world and causes us to marvel at and worship God. Pressing the dirt over seedlings in the garden, watching the sunrise while you sip your coffee, or simply taking a hike at a local park instills awe for the majesty and greatness of God. The psalmist writes, "When I look at your heavens, the work of your fingers, the moon and the stars, which you have set in place, what is man that you are mindful of him, and the son of man that you care for him?"[4] As Gospel Moms, we need this reminder to reorient our minds and hearts around what is true. Nature deepens our appreciation of the fact that the God who made the mountains and seas and canyons is the same God who knit us in our own mother's womb. Here are some ways to practice the habit of nature:

- Round up the family, and head to a local park to walk.

- Make a picnic out of a meal you usually eat inside.

- Look up a state or national park, and go camping or even just bring a lunch and do a day trip.

- Take the family outside after dark. If you can't see the stars from your home, head outside of town to get a view.

---

[4] Psalm 8:3-4.

WE REORIENT OUR MINDS & HEARTS AROUND WHAT IS TRUE.

- Grow something. Whether it's in a pot on a small porch or an expansive cut flower garden, find a plant to tend and watch grow.

- Wake up early one morning to watch the sunrise. Don't look through a window; go outside for the best view.

Habit of Rest

Sabbath is one of those terms that many of us have heard and maybe even use, but it still feels like an enigma. When we hear about the Sabbath as a "day of rest," we mothers cock our heads and wonder, *How on earth can I rest as a mom?* But thinking of the Sabbath only as a day to "not work" limits the view of what we're offered. The Sabbath is the fourth of the Ten Commandments. The reason given is simple: "For the Lord made the heavens and the earth, the sea, and everything in them in six days; then he rested on the seventh day. Therefore the Lord blessed the Sabbath day and declared it holy."[5] This points us back to the creation account—you can't even get two pages into the Bible before you see the Sabbath. God, after creating the heavens and the earth and everything in it, rested. Not because he was tired but because he had completed his good work. The Bible tells us that God set the example of the Sabbath for humankind so that we would learn to rest in his goodness and work before we start our own. When we rest, we remember how powerful and all-sufficient God is and who we are in him. We can bask in God's glory rather than "being" and "doing" and "accomplishing." More than anything, rest is a state of the heart.

Because of the person and work of Christ, we can have spiritual rest. No matter what we're facing, we can focus on our delight and joy in him and his accomplished work, not our own. Christians may not all agree on whether we should set aside an entire day, as the Israelites did, but we all acknowledge the principle that God commands we rest for our good and his glory. Just like God wanted to remind the Israelites that they were no longer slaves

---

[5] Exodus 20:11 CSB.

to Egypt or their pagan gods, he wants us to remember that our lives and choices should not be dictated by work, fashion, social media, our homes, our children's demands, our in-laws' preferences, or our own sinful desires. We are daughters of the Most High. God is our deliverer. And now, we freely walk in the Spirit that lives in us because of Jesus's sacrifice on our behalf.

When this gets under your skin, you can be free of the constant need to achieve and produce and start to value the God-given gift of rest. Whether that's prioritizing a good night's sleep instead of staying up too late, resting from screens or media, or taking a full day off your traditional work so that you can enjoy something fun and think about the Lord, there are many ways to practice rest as a mom!

- Take time to study passages of Scripture that talk about the Sabbath or the general idea of rest. This will help you understand what types of rest are available to you and why God designed this as an important pattern of life.

- Pick a day or even a couple of hours each week where you'd like to set aside some of your normal work and do something that helps you focus on who God is and enjoy the good gifts he's given you. (Hint: This could even be laying aside the laundry basket and just freely swinging in the hammock in the backyard, enjoying the sunshine and your kids with no pressure to multitask!)

- Take time to do some things that move you to worship. This might be taking a walk, spending time with friends, or practicing a hobby like painting, sewing, basketball, or writing.

- Focus on your sleep. Even though moms don't always have control over nighttime wakings and feedings, what can you do to prioritize healthy sleep habits?

- Take a digital detox by setting aside your phone for certain parts of the day or a day each week—or even taking a break from social media.

Habit of Care

In our modern age, a stereotypical picture of a mom is a woman who has dark circles under her eyes and wears a messy topknot and sweats. She's exhausted and worn out, sitting curled up on a couch nursing a cup of coffee while watching her kids play in the living room. Yet this picture is a stereotype for a reason—it was us for a time, and we're betting it's been (or is) many of you. There's no doubt about it: Motherhood is exhausting. Sleepless nights, long days, and demands more frequent than most of us have ever experienced—we can barely do our hair in the morning without being interrupted. In this season, many of us fall into the trap of believing, *If I just read my Bible and pray, I'll be fine. Christ will supply everything I need.* On one level, this is true. God does care for us in the most deep and ultimate way. But God also made us embodied beings—both body *and* soul—which means both need care.

We've always been struck by how when Paul is in prison, he asks Timothy to bring him his cloak, his books, and his parchments—a request for small, seemingly insignificant comforts that made it into the holy Scriptures.[6] But this is what it means to be an embodied being with needs and limits. Alongside prayer, Scripture, and church, we need food, water, sleep, and rest. In his kindness, God made it so that having a cup of tea in the afternoon would bring comfort, sitting down to eat a meal instead of standing at the counter would be refreshing, and taking a bath before bed would bring relaxation to our weary bodies.

Self-care is a term fraught with assumptions and misunderstandings, but at its heart and from a biblical viewpoint, it doesn't have to mean self-indulgence. It can be a good gift from a loving Father to remind us we are not self-sufficient and only dependent on ourselves. Here are a few ideas on ways to get started with the habit of care:

---

[6] 2 Timothy 4:13.

- Examine how much physical activity you're getting. As much as possible, move your body each day, even for a walk or stretching routine.

- Evaluate your nutrition. Eat foods that nourish and energize your body—not just the kids' leftovers. Consider if you need vitamins or other supplements to help round out your nutrition.

- If you're energized by spending time with people, gather with a few friends. If you're energized by being alone, spend time in solitude, journaling, praying, or even just thinking.

- Consider which small things (like that cup of tea) comfort and revitalize you, and make them part of your routine.

- Consider counseling. Don't let issues go unresolved. If needed, explore your options for therapy, or find a wise friend you can talk with regularly.

Don't Ignore Your Limits

In all these practices, there's one common thread of reality: We're humans with limitations. While our children may believe that mothers can fix any problem, can solve any puzzle, and actually have eyes in the back of our heads, we would attest that there is no greater reality check on our limitations than what motherhood brings. Our limitations can feel frustrating, but they're actually wonderfully designed by God. Before the Fall, Adam and Eve were limited. They each had one body, in one place, at one time. Because of this, we know that many of our limitations are not due to sin. Even Jesus, the perfect human, had limits. He didn't heal every person, preach to every crowd, or teach every disciple. In fact, as his ministry grew, causing him to be busier and busier, we actually saw him draw more boundaries, getting away to be alone with his Father and pray. Jesus didn't do it all, and we shouldn't (and can't!) either.

Our limitations are not to be ignored or trampled on but actually serve as a guide to living as a Gospel Mom. Limitations remind us of who we are and who God is. We are needy, dependent, fragile people; he is the all-powerful, almighty, ever-present, utterly holy King of the world and God of the universe. What a comfort to our motherhood! Our weary souls can rest because he already completed the ultimate work: his sacrifice on the cross. The habits we implement in motherhood are physical representations of our spiritual reality. They give us space to slow down and cultivate our love for God and our love for our neighbors. These habits are not to create a works-based, whitewashed-tomb Pharisee.[7] They're to cultivate a sustainable life for a mom who wants to follow Jesus until the end of her days. She doesn't have to do them; she *gets* to do them. They are the still waters and pleasant boundary lines of the abundant life.

[7] Matthew 23:27.

PART 3

THE THINKING

THE THINKING

Fair warning: This section is going to get a little wild. But it's also the fun part. It's where the freedom and joy and power of gospel motherhood really start to take shape and have a tangible impact on your mom life. At the same time, this is probably the part that feels the hardest to get your arms around—at least it is for us! Even after years of practice, we need reminders to slow down and consider each of these areas as the Lord leads. We titled this portion "The Thinking" because it's going to require just that: lots of thinking!

In this portion of the book we're going to consider our unique cirumstances, personal conscience, and heart motivations.

All three of these things work in tandem with what we discussed in parts 1 and 2 of this book. The CFRC framework, combined with personal study of Scripture and cultivation of the spiritual disciplines and habits we discussed, provide the essential foundation that will help each mom make gospel-based decisions in her own life. Consider the three topics in this section almost like knowing the type and quantity of spices to use when cooking. They're all important elements to use as you apply the gospel to motherhood. Sometimes there will be decisions or seasons where you emphasize one topic or area more than another or where one feels more important or impactful than another. Just like we talked about with various spiritual disciplines and habits, God may even inspire you to hone in on these one at a time as the Holy Spirit brings different things to mind to shape your heart and thinking to be more like him. Our biggest caution is to not think of the topics in this section as linear steps to work through or as traditional building blocks that you set up in order (1, then 2, then 3, and so on). Instead, the elements in this section will play together as you think through a decision to discover not just what God wants you to do but who he wants you to be.

Essentially, we're going to give you a flyover of how to understand biblical wisdom. Biblical wisdom is knowing how to apply the truths, commands, and principles revealed in God's Word to our own lives and circumstances. When you face a situation that's not spelled out in Scripture, wisdom is knowing what actions and attitudes would best align with God's character and commands, then acting on them. We admit, this work is complex and hard. Like we said, it takes thinking! It takes combining all that God is teaching you as you abide in his Word, go to church or studies, talk with friends and mentors, reflect on your lived experiences, and prayerfully ask the Lord to show you the right way forward.

But remember, God doesn't just care about the outward "right decisions" (although they are important!); he also cares about who we are along the way—the *how* and *why* behind our decisions. Are we making decisions and acting out of love? Worship? Humility? Service? Are we making decisions wisely and prayerfully? Are we being patient and self-controlled as we do things? Or are we approaching life with a chip on our shoulder—with pride, self-sufficiency, and a sense that we already know what's best? Are we judgmental and cocky about knowing the "right answers," snubbing our nose at someone who seems to still be learning?

A Gospel Mom thinks about not just what God wants her to do but who he wants her to be. What good is it if you make all the "right decisions" on the outside to fit a mold of Christian motherhood but your heart is far from God and you're not really walking in faith?[1] Just as we've repeated throughout this

---

[1] Matthew 16:26.

book, God isn't asking you to know every answer or make perfect decisions every time. He's asking for you to soften your heart to him in the process and trust him to guide you.

After we dive deep into some of the components of biblical wisdom in these next few chapters through considering our unique circumstances, personal conscience, and heart motivations, we'll wrap up by discussing how we interact with other moms. While the first three chapters will zero in on you and your personal decisions as a mom, we also want to explore how we consider others, remembering that this life isn't just about our own decisions or desires—we're a part of God's family, and we're swept up into the larger story of God's plan. That reality might require us to sacrifice, show deference, or make changes at times as we seek to love, serve, and live in community with other moms.

Obedience to God is evidence of a heart that has been redeemed. Though we won't be able to obey God perfectly in this life, and we'll continually stumble and struggle, our faith should produce actions and words that reflect Christ more and more over the course of our lives. Look to the letters in the New Testament. Many of them follow similar patterns. First, the writer praises and recounts what Jesus did on his people's behalf, and then the writer switches gears to share the implications of Jesus's work on the lives of those of the church the letter is written to, often using transition words like *therefore*. Essentially, the message is this: **Because** Jesus saved you from death and gave you new life, **now** you should think and act in a new way. You are free from old patterns or cultural norms and expectations to follow God. The point isn't that we make perfect decisions or understand everything about ourselves but that we are always looking to the one who is perfect and seeking to understand the Lord's will as we know it today.

Remember that God is using your life for his important kingdom purposes. He's not going to abandon you now as you consider what he wants for your life as a Gospel Mom.

CHAPTER 7

UNIQUE CIRCUMSTANCES

Picture that good ole Venn diagram from elementary school. Right in the middle, where the circles overlap, we see that as moms, we have a lot of things in common— we have shared experiences and fears, and we cross common milestones and ask similar questions. In many ways, it feels like we have a shared language and a shared heart. This is why a mom who is a complete stranger can post about her birth story or her child's diagnosis online, and even though we don't know her, our hearts empathize.

The same is true for us as Christians. We all worship the same triune God. We listen to and submit our lives to the same holy Word. We share the same church history and are united into the same family. We share one faith and one baptism. We have the same Spirit living inside of us, guiding us as we obey the same commands and live according to the same big-*T* Truth. There is incredible unity in our mission, our calling, and the way we ought to live as Christians.

And yet on the outer sides of that diagram, there's a myriad of differences to take into account. Though it's good and important for us to focus on unity and sameness, failing to also appreciate the unique things about our lives and circumstances might mean we're not able to treat one another with understanding and compassion. We might not encourage or support one another as we ought. We might grow deeply discouraged and frustrated with ourselves as we try to conform our motherhood to look like someone else's. And most importantly, we might miss the beauty and complexity of God's glory being displayed through his people and in his kingdom. We might think that the diamond just has one flat side instead of multiple facets that, when turned and examined, reflect the light in much more awe-inspiring ways.

When we think about all that God has for us in motherhood, we need an understanding and appreciation of both the ways he's called us to the same mission and the ways he's leading us to live that out differently. Understanding how God's Word and the gospel come to bear on our lives is what biblical wisdom and decision-making are all about. And this starts by looking at and thinking about our unique circumstances. What are the facts of our situation—the realities about who we are, where we live, and what needs and resources we have available? How do we ask not just *What has God given her?* but also *What has God given me?* Take it from our own personal experience; we've had plenty of missteps trying to conform our lives to look like our "ideal mom" or our friends, only to realize that God was doing something different in our motherhood—showing us what it meant to be gentle, patient, kind, or nurturing in a way that might yield different choices from another mom.

Let's explore some of the aspects of a mom's life or circumstances that might impact the way she applies God's Word and gospel principles to her situation.

Who You Are

When we consider who we are as Gospel Moms and how God is working in and through us, we ought to consider the life story that he's written and is writing for us. No two stories are going to be the same, and that's not only okay but also the way he's designed it. We all tend to have a sense of our own personality or default mode of thinking and operating. Are you more "get things done" or more "sit back and enjoy"? Are you more vocal, emotive, and extroverted, or are you more quiet, stoic, and introverted? Are you good at strategizing and keeping ahold of the big picture, or are you detail oriented and careful with small things? These aren't right or wrong or good or bad things; they are just realities about the way we're designed. We can't be all things, but who God made us plays into what faithfulness and gospel obedience look like in our lives.

Psalm 139 paints a beautiful picture of God's intentionality when forming each person and life. He knits us together in the womb and carefully, thoughtfully, and purposefully forms our genetic code. We are all impacted by the Fall in some way, and God in his wisdom allows and sovereignly determines what things might become challenges for us in the way we are formed and developed. But the Word says that God knows all our days before they begin and that we each have a special, God-given ability to image him in the way he designed us.

Theologians along with psychologists, sociologists, and neurologists all have different theories about how our personalities are formed—and it's clear that it's through some combination of our genetic code, our family of origin, the environment we're raised in, the life experiences we have, the hurts and traumas we face, and the way our faith intersects that along the way. While the Lord and his Spirit certainly have the power to trump or instantly heal any wound, genetic abnormality, or thought pattern, in most cases, he works in and through these things for our ultimate good and his glory as we live our mission in his kingdom. He brings beauty and redemption from the ashes and the broken places, leading to a life that notices and seeks out different hurts, gifts, and needs in others.

Similarly, we can start to understand how the challenges, sufferings, wounds, or traumas we've faced might impact our motherhood. Sometimes these things can be overcome and nearly fully healed. Sometimes they're tender wounds and scars that tear back open with various triggers like hidden landmines in our daily lives and relationships. Other times these wounds

NO TWO STORIES ARE GOING TO BE THE SAME.

can mean significant limitations for our health and capacity, or they can become catalysts for service and advocacy for others. In all of these things, it's worth thinking about how suffering and hardship might come to bear on your decisions as you seek to follow God in your mothering.

Consider a few other ways that who you are and where you came from play into how you mother. This isn't meant to be an exhaustive list, just some questions to give you some idea of the vast and varied elements that make you who you are:

- How many years have you been a believer, and what is your personal journey of faith and your testimony of Jesus's work in your life?

- What is your personal experience with church or Christian culture? (This probably shapes your approach to spiritual disciplines and habits, sharing the gospel, and integrating your faith into your marriage and motherhood.)

- What was your journey to motherhood? For example:

    Did you enter motherhood via an unexpected pregnancy?

    Were you single?

    Were you married? If so, were you married happily, or was your marriage under some strain?

    Were you afraid of motherhood or excited about it?

    Did this journey to motherhood come after a past abortion?

- Do you or did you have a good or bad relationship with your own mom and dad?

- Do you come from a blended family and/or did you watch your own parents go through relational trauma?

- What aspects of your childhood were healthy, and what are things you don't want to repeat?

- How are your physical health and mental health?

  Do you have an acute or chronic health challenge?

  Do you have pain or disease?

  Are you neurodivergent or neurotypical?

  Have you had mental health struggles such as PPD/PPA or a diagnosis of something like obsessive compulsive disorder or bipolar disorder?

- What are your particular habitual temptations or struggles?

  Do you have a history of addiction?

  Have you struggled in the past or currently with tobacco, drugs, or alcohol abuse? Pornography or erotica? Addictions to gambling, food, shopping, media, and so on?

Your answers to these questions and more will shape the way you approach motherhood, but they don't have the final word on who you are or how you can serve in God's kingdom. Just as soon as we learn to live in the story God has written for us, we also must depend on him in faith, knowing that God is not limited by our circumstances or personality. Just because we grew up in a lonely home doesn't mean we can't create a warm, nurturing home for our own children. Ponder the truths about your life, and also entrust them to the Lord. He can do more than you could ever hope or imagine, making you new in him.

Your Spouse

If you're married,[1] then you can probably remember the covenant you made before God and others as you vowed, "Till death do us part." Next to yourself, your husband is probably the person that you know the most

---

[1] We recognize that not all moms are married. If you are a single mom, this will impact your life circumstances and how you make decisions. If reading this portion feels painful or unhelpful, feel free to skip to the next section.

intimately. After a few years, you've seen each other at your best and at your worst. You've shared finances, a comforter, and maybe even a toothbrush in a pinch. And everything you do as a married couple and as parents impacts each other. Hopefully, you've learned that things work best when you have shared values, are on the same page, and are both pulling in the same direction.

Yet marriage and parenting rarely go that smoothly. There are kinks to work out, communication patterns to improve, and areas where the Fall still darkens the relationship. When it comes to being a Gospel Mom and understanding how God wants you to mother, that reality is not considered in a vacuum. It's essentially and intimately connected to your husband and how he's called to father—how you *collectively* are working together according to God's Word to raise up your children in the Lord.

This means that who your husband is—his strengths, weaknesses, interests, leanings, and preferences—must play into your motherhood. We're to seek unity with our husbands as we move forward and make decisions in parenting.[2] God didn't just give children to their mothers, for them to call all the shots while their dads sit on the sidelines—he gave them to their mothers *and their fathers.*

Seeking to understand, respect, and come alongside your husband in parenting and life decisions does not mean seeking his permission every time you open the snack drawer, and it doesn't mean having cookie-cutter or stereotypical roles or delegation of tasks between husband and wife. It simply means that to have a healthy, loving marriage, you want to know your husband and listen to his wisdom, insight, and preferences—just like how he should be listening and responding to you and your expertise. You both prioritize unity together, making choices that might even feel sacrificial to one of you in the name of furthering the gospel and loving each other well.

Perhaps your husband feels strongly about a particular schooling choice

---

[2] 1 Corinthians 13:4-7; Genesis 2:24; Ephesians 5:22-24.

or he's sensing a call toward overseas missions. Maybe he's passionate about adoption or he's interested in the idea of a larger-than-average family. Maybe your husband works long hours, or maybe he's highly involved in family life and has a flexible schedule. He could be a man who loves to cook or organize the house. Whatever it is, our husbands' desires and preferences should play a crucial role in the way we live our lives and motherhood. Regardless of the specifics, as you honor your own husband, it should shape your motherhood in ways that look different from other moms. Each married couple will seek to apply God's words with wisdom to their own family's unique dynamics.

And finally, some of you have husbands who aren't believers, are functional unbelievers (even if they go to church), or aren't fully aligned with what you think God's Word says in a certain area. You face a completely different set of challenges. Perhaps your life and motherhood look different from your ideal as you pray and live out a long-suffering kind of love.[3] In these cases, to know what to do takes tremendous care and wisdom along with helpful insight from mentors, pastors, and even counselors.

Regardless of the specifics of your situation, the point stands: Your spouse—who they are, what they are like, and what they desire for your children—is going to impact the way you live out your unique gospel motherhood.

Your Family Makeup

If there weren't enough variables to consider already, now we're getting into the household itself. How many kids you have, how far apart they are spaced, and their personalities and unique needs are all going to impact the decisions you make as a mom. A mom of seven with three older children (ages 16, 14, and 12) who can help with her younger four (ages 8, 6, 4, and 2)

---

[3] We mean long-suffering in the biblical sense of patient endurance, not in terms of suffering physical, emotional, or sexual abuse. If abuse or other illegal or illicit behavior is occurring in your marriage, please tell someone and reach out for counsel and/or professional intervention.

is going to have different resources and challenges than a mom to four under age 5, one of whom has Down syndrome. One situation isn't objectively "easier" than the other, but these different resources and challenges will yield different solutions and biblical applications. The mom of seven might rarely need outside-of-the-family childcare while she runs errands or pursues hobbies, while the mother of four might stay at home plus need the help of a part-time nanny as she juggles therapies, doctor's appointments, and young children with high levels of needs.

Sometimes when we start to feel judgmental and condemning of other moms' choices (or of our own—*I mean, why is this so hard for me but not for her?*), we're not considering the way our household and family dynamics differ. Sometimes we're looking at a mom who has all school-age children, and we're pining to prioritize exercise as she does, but we're forgetting that we have two kids in diapers who are up multiple times a night, and that that regimented workout schedule just wouldn't make sense for our family's needs right now. Sometimes when we're thinking about family traditions, and we're not understanding why the complex craft our mom did with us at Easter doesn't translate to our own family, we're forgetting that our family of origin had three girls spaced three years apart, not four boys spaced two years apart.

Not only are we each dealing with different quantities, ages, and genders of children, but some of us might also be caring for children who are fostered or adopted. Some of you might have one or more children with a disability, a severe illness, or life-threatening allergies. Each child's needs, concerns, and personality are going to play into your choices about childcare, discipline, special activities, screen-time limits, schooling, medical care, and more.

Where You Live

Just like Paul notes in many of his epistles, the gospel (though universally applicable and true) plays itself out differently in the context of different cultures and people groups. The same is true for us today. What nation we live in, what culture we grow up in, and what subculture we socialize in with friends, church, and family all impact what decisions we make in motherhood. Whether we live in a rural community, an urban area, a suburb, or somewhere in between, our setting affects what challenges and options are available to us. Sometimes the norms and options of our local community aren't wise, and we need to steer away from them and understand how they are shaping us in ways that aren't aligned with God's Word. But in other cases, those norms are just the reality about where we live, and we must seek to live faithfully in the midst of them.

If we live in the cornfields of Iowa, it can be hard to put ourselves in the shoes of a mom living in downtown Los Angeles, or Boston, or Australia, or South Korea. It can be hard to imagine what choices and challenges she might face—what options she has that we don't have or how her lifestyle and gospel application are impacted by where she lives. For a mom in a Western, developed nation with a lot of political freedom, it could be hard to understand why a Christian mom is doing something different in a country where there is a significant risk of making certain parenting decisions or where she doesn't have access to some of the same resources. God isn't calling us to assess our lives based on someone else's geograpy, but to consider what life looks life in the town and street where God has placed us.

The Things You Care About

Our life experiences, the places where we live and work, the things we know and have learned about, and the issues that people around us are facing come together and turn our shoulders toward certain needs and issues, allowing us to see and relate to some things more easily than others. This is God designed! Not only does he determine the time and place where each person will live for his glory and purposes, but he uses the unique and varied interests of his children to help minister to the wide variety of needs across the globe. It's good that not all Christian moms are called to or are interested in the same things or are mothering the same way.

We should consider the role we play in God's kingdom and the specific areas of knowledge, experience, and interest that he's placed in our lives. This concept is evident in the New Testament when Paul talks about the fact that the Spirit has gifted people in the church with different things for the edification of the body of Christ. For the two of us (Emily and Laura), that's included writing and speaking because those are unique skills and desires that the Lord has placed on our hearts—but not every mom should use written or verbal communication online as a mechanism for reaching others with the gospel. We also both feel inclined toward speaking about disability because we both have a child with a disability. Just because that's an area of emphasis that we both like to give time, money, and attention to doesn't mean that every mom has to adopt that as her "issue."

You have the freedom to think through your own life circumstances and consider areas of ministry or emphasis that God has called you to. Discovering this will also help you make decisions about how the gospel comes to bear in your life, particularly as you think about the Redemption piece of the gospel framework. It can help you figure out how to spend your time and energy and where to focus. And it's an area that will likely make your life look different from the lives of the moms around you—and that's a beautiful thing! Just because we care deeply about a topic doesn't mean we should expect other moms must do the same or deem them unloving, unwise, or ineffective for the kingdom if they do differently.

Here's what we mean. Perhaps you feel a huge pull toward hospitality, and it's relatively easy for you to open your home. You love being the house on the block that pulls people together, offering meals and snacks and staying up late to talk on the driveway. But that doesn't make every other family on the block wrong for not emphasizing hospitality in the same way. Maybe another mom on the same street finds it hard to host frequently because she cares for her kids and holds a part-time job at the local pro-life women's clinic, where she loves sharing the gospel with moms-to-be who feel vulnerable and unsupported. Perhaps your neighbor next door doesn't host often because she and her husband are currently fostering two children who need more boundaries and safety within their four walls in order to have safe attachments. It wouldn't be wise for them to let people come and go. In all of these cases, these moms are showing different versions of hospitality, even if it doesn't look like it traditionally does. Each mom is leaning into her area of interest and life circumstances in ministry—and they all play out differently. They can't—and shouldn't—equally care about and devote time to the exact same things with the same intensity.

Your Season of Life

Finally, when it comes to considering what gospel motherhood looks like and how you're going to apply the things you're learning in God's Word, it's important to consider what season you're in. Just like the climate goes through annual shifts in winter, spring, summer, and fall, we go through different seasons of life. Winter is a time for plants to lay dormant and the earth to rest while it prepares for cultivation and planting, and you might be walking through a stage of life that is colder, harder, and less active and productive than you would like. While the word *season* can feel like Christianese or get overused, it truly is a biblical way to think about the fact that not everything in life needs to or can happen at one time or in the same season. "There is an occasion for everything, and a time for every activity under heaven…a time to weep and a time to laugh; a time to mourn and a time to dance…a time to embrace and a time to avoid embracing."[4]

The way you apply the gospel when you're in "the little years" is likely going to look different from the way you apply it when you have teenagers, even though the overarching principles are the same. The choices you might need to make when you have an ailing parent and elementary schoolers to care for are likely going to be different from what you needed to do when your parent was able to help and offer practical support in your daily

---

[4] Ecclesiastes 3:1-8 csb.

life. You might also go through seasons where you have a child receiving a diagnosis or needing treatment for mental health struggles. You may have a season where marriage is easy and fun and a season where it's not only dull, but it's taking a lot of commitment and work. You may have a season where you're able to volunteer three days a week at church, organizing Bible studies and small groups, and then another season where you're barely able to be involved at all.

Understanding and accepting the ebb and flow of seasons—along with the different joys, freedoms, limitations, and challenges they present—can be difficult, but it's also very helpful as we consider what it means to live our calling as Gospel Moms in whatever circumstances the Lord has given us.

Even Jesus Didn't Do Everything He Possibly Could Have

We're going to keep diving into the concept of gospel thinking and decision-making and all the factors that play into that, but before we move forward, we wanted to pause and reiterate that even though, as moms, we're really hard on ourselves for not being able to do it all and be it all, our finitude is okay. In this social media world, we can open apps and see moms in different locations, in different seasons, and with different backgrounds, interests, and skills living out motherhood in ways that look beautiful, fulfilling, and appealing. Just as soon as we've decided that we want to be a free-range parenting mom, we can see someone online who focuses her whole life and parenting method on health and fitness or who gives much of her energy to the advocacy of a certain issue, and we start to question ourselves and flounder. *Should we be caring about all of those things too? Have we chosen the right way of life?*

That's why it's so important that we devote ourselves not to a certain method or identity but to Christ himself and the unchanging identity we have in him. He cares about what kind of mom we are as we evaluate our circumstances and move forward—and he wants us to order our priorities after his. This means that we can hold things loosely and be responsive to his leading in our lives, clinging not to our plans but to his will. Because no matter what circumstances he brings, he will lead us to follow him and reflect him in the midst of those. We can acknowledge our hopes and desires for the way we thought things would be but evaluate and accept the life that God has actually given us, the place we actually live, and the family we actually have. We don't live in the "what-ifs." We live our motherhood in the "what is."

It should cause us to take heart when we realize that during his earthly ministry, Jesus also had limitations and followed the will of his Father. He did not address all issues in all places all at one time. In fact, he still has work to come back and do![5] He lived and moved and traveled to different locations where he ministered to the people who needed him there—in that time and in that moment. And even then, he didn't heal every single person who wanted or needed healing. Nor did he answer every question that was asked. Additionally, he had seasons of life—as a child, he invested time learning and growing up into knowledge of God and his Word.[6] As a young adult, he worked as a carpenter and spent his days making a living.[7] And late in his life, he had a season of active "public" ministry where he revealed who he was and completed his work at that time on earth, dying on the cross and rising from the dead. If it was okay for our Savior to have different seasons and stages of his life, for him to respond to the Father's leading and discern what God wanted him to do each day, then this is certainly okay for us. Similarly, Jesus's earliest disciples and apostles went on to serve different people groups, start churches in different areas, and complete different tasks related to the spread of the gospel. This wasn't a sign that someone was doing it wrong; it was a sign of something healthy and right.

---

[5] Hebrews 9:28.

[6] Luke 2:40, 49, 52.

[7] Mark 6:3.

The same is true for us. Though we should each seek to prayerfully and wisely evaluate how to make the best use of our time and resources in motherhood, we shouldn't consider ourselves automatically "wrong" for living our lives differently from the other moms in our church or community (let alone those we see on social media). Your unique life and experience of motherhood can be lived to God's glory, and that's a "win" for the kingdom.

CHAPTER 8

PERSONAL CONSCIENCE

H ave you ever heard a Christian speaker or leader say things like, "That's a gray area!" or "That's something the Bible doesn't prescribe," or "We have freedom in Christ here." They're likely addressing topics like where to spend your volunteer time, what kind of vacations to take, what movie to show at a birthday party, what types of medication or therapies to provide for your children, or when to give your kids cell phones. These are all things that if you searched for the words in Scripture, you'd come up with zero results. That's because these are areas where the Bible doesn't give exact rules, directions, or instructions.

In a sense, there is much "Christian freedom" in how we go about these decisions, and for most issues, there isn't one right way for all Christians for all of time. But it also doesn't mean "Do whatever you want! Truth is relative!" And if you're anything like us, you've still wondered if some methods in motherhood are more biblical and holy than others (like some online mom sources claim), and you've thought, *If there is a "most God-honoring" way to do something, as Christian moms, we want that one!*

As we've discussed in previous chapters, God does have clear laws and commands, he has a good design for our daily lives, and he cares about what we do. He has revealed wisdom for life in his Word. As moms who follow Christ, we desire to align our lives with this, not to just go our own way. So the question becomes, *If God's Word isn't prescriptive about a topic, how do we know what's right?* There are many facets to this answer as we seek to employ biblical wisdom, including listening to the Word of God, the leading of the Holy Spirit in our lives, and the wise counsel of others. But there is another important factor at play we want to explore. Enter your personal conscience.

Your conscience is your personal sense of right and wrong. It's often an intangible feeling you have in situations about what you should or shouldn't do. Some people refer to it as a "moral compass." It isn't a Magic 8 Ball or some outside voice like Jiminy Cricket nervously following you around. Rather, your conscience is a gift from God that can help guide your choices but not make them perfectly. It's like a yellow flag waving at you to say, "Hey! Something inside of you feels like this is wrong. Why is that?" When it fires, it doesn't always mean your choice *is* wrong, but it's a good indicator to go back and understand something about what you believe and why. *Where did this idea about life and motherhood come from?*

As we dig into this concept, we're going to examine how our personal conscience is formed, how we can further align it to the Word of God and the Holy Spirit's leading in our lives, and how to make decisions in faith as we understand our personal belief system and seek to glorify God.

How the Personal Conscience Is Formed

If you have siblings, have you ever spent time reminiscing about your childhood together? Perhaps a major life event will come up and one of you remembers it vividly, yet another doesn't remember it at all. Or maybe you each remember different things about the same memory. It's like how the old saying goes: "There's your truth, my truth, and the Truth." Just like we explored in the previous chapter, one of the incredible parts about God's design is that while all humans were made in his image, no two people are exactly alike. The personal conscience is called "personal" for a reason—it's as individual and unique as you are and is influenced by a huge variety of factors. These are just a few:

- the time in history you've been placed in
- the culture you were born into and raised in

- your family of origin's rules, personalities, values, and tendencies
- your relationships with your siblings, friends, and/or spouse
- your personality and disposition
- your personal hurts or traumas
- your socioeconomic status and the "class" you were raised in
- your education, including specific curriculum or schooling values
- your denomination or particular sect of Christianity
- your understanding of what God's Word says is right and wrong
- your values, hobbies, talents, and fears

Knowing how varied our experiences and circumstances are, we can see how different moms might come to different conclusions about gray areas in life. Our life experiences and proclivities shape our whole belief system about motherhood—what we care about, what we prioritize, and what we proselytize to other moms. It forms what we believe a "good mom" does and what the "right decisions" are in motherhood. It often comes out in statements like, "I'll never let my kids throw a tantrum in the grocery store!" (This is, of course, said before she has kids. Bless her heart.) It's how we seek to fill in that blank line before *mom* and how we shape our handbook for motherhood. It might look like this:

- A mom who had health struggles and experienced healing through a change in her nutrition may have strong feelings about what she feeds her family. Eating nonorganic or processed foods might seem "wrong" to her.

- A mom who had a negative experience with homeschooling growing up may go on to feel that homeschooling is a "bad" choice because of what she endured.

- A mom who fondly remembers annual family vacations at

national parks might feel as though she's failing as a mom if she doesn't re-create those same experiences for her children. When she instead books a vacation to the beach, she feels that it's "wrong" or, at the very least, not the "right" choice.

- A mom who experienced a childhood where there was no monitoring of media and still can't shake some of the memories of what she saw might implement strong house rules around media choices. Her conscience fires "no, no, no!" any time her children ask to go outside of her tightly laid boundaries.

All of these moms are making choices that they believe are best for their families—and that's a good place to start! And ultimately, there's nothing inherently wrong with being cautious about nutrition, choosing a different form of schooling than homeschooling, taking a vacation every summer, or carefully monitoring our children's media. All of those are choices a mom is free to make! Yet our call as Christians (not just as moms) is to understand what we believe qualifies as best and ask if that aligns with the Word of God. And we're to consider not just the actual decision but why we've made it, how tightly we hold it, and how much we try to convert others to our way of thinking or judge others for making different choices.

Troubleshooting Your Own Conscience

As we consider how our own beliefs about motherhood have formed and shaped our view of what's right and wrong,[1] we might run into some bumps. In fact, most of us start our motherhood journey with "conscience issues," and God goes to work in our hearts, helping us better align with his Word. Paul refers to these issues as a "weak conscience."[2] A weak conscience is one that is influenced by sin or holds fast to rules and regulations that are not

---

[1] See appendix B for more information on weak and strong consciences.

[2] 1 Corinthians 8:7-12 NIV; also Romans 14.

universally binding for all Christians. This can happen through an overly sensitive conscience or a seared conscience.

An Overly Sensitive Conscience

While it's good to have a tender and soft heart toward God and be sensitive to what he says is right and wrong, in some areas our consciences can be overly sensitive or hyperactive. We can start creating rules or laws that God's Word hasn't put in place and aren't universal for all of God's people.

For example, the mom who doesn't want to homeschool and feels that it is "bad" might have an overly sensitive conscience if she can't see that her negative experience with homeschooling doesn't mean the choice to homeschool is—in and of itself—a doctrinal error or sin against God. This is especially true if her feeling that "it's an unacceptable option" extends to everyone.

Or the mom who cares deeply about her family's nutrition might have a hyperactive conscience if she feels disgusted by or verbally condemns other moms when they pick up fast food for their family for dinner. In these instances, a mom (unknowingly or not) has elevated her personal conscience to be superior to God's Word as she seeks to dictate others' consciences—and actions.

Those with a weak conscience tend to have a fearful or legalistic bent, putting themselves in the seat of judge and jury in areas where there is actually freedom in God's commands and laws.

A Seared Conscience

Our consciences can also be dulled or damaged. In 1 Timothy 4:2, Paul refers to this as a "seared" conscience, which happens when we ignore our personal conscience and become desensitized to what is right and wrong. If we feel our conscience tugging on our hearts but don't seek to understand it, we're in danger of quieting its voice as we engage in sin (sometimes in the name of Christian liberty). For example, we may have a glass of wine on the weekends, then start to have one every evening—and perhaps there, our conscience is waving the flag, but we ignore it—and soon we're having two or three glasses each night and feeling like we need it to survive this motherhood gig. We don't really feel bad about it or realize that this is a problem because we've dulled the warning of our Spirit-taught conscience.

A dull or seared conscience puts us in danger of falling into sinful habits and not actually feeling all that bad about it because the voice of our conscience has grown dim as we stuffed it down over and over again.

Freeing Our Conscience

There is good news for both of these "weak consciences": Our conscience can also be freed or changed when we pause to understand our thinking. We can look underneath our beliefs and ask, *Why do I feel so strongly about this? Is this an area commanded by God that I need to confess sin, repent, and change in? Or is it a belief system I acquired over the years, brought on by personal experiences or cultural standards? Do I need to unbind my conscience on this topic?* How will we find the answers? Through a combination of things. Here are a few:

- Study God's Word, growing in knowledge and discernment of his laws and loves. (Hint: This is what we overviewed in part 1 of this book—see how all the aspects of this book tie together? When we understand his design and his story, we're equipped to see how our belief systems do or do not align with God's.)

- Gain a grasp on important spiritual disciplines and habits for the Christian. (Hint: In part 2, we talked about how these disciplines and habits help us have regular time for prayer and reading the Word so we can bring our questions about matters of conscience to God.)

- Discuss and practice discipleship with more mature believers. Wise mentors often have a broader perspective on life and can help us sift through our beliefs.

- Pray for the Holy Spirit to guide and convict us.

- Be part of a local church where we can study the Bible together and observe other beliefs and other Christian moms, seeing how they may be faithfully living out the gospel differently and challenging or affirming our own beliefs.

- Reflect on our own life experiences and gain wisdom as we observe the fruit of our belief systems.

If we earnestly seek the Lord for an answer to our feelings about what's "right and wrong" in our motherhood, he will be faithful in helping us understand it and walk in freedom.

Obedient, but Humbly Evaluating

But what about times when we're not sure what our conscience is saying? Sometimes we think we have a strong conviction, but we're not sure if we should be open to other options. For example, allowing your children to trick-or-treat. You may feel strongly that Halloween isn't something you want to allow your children to participate in—in any form or fashion. Yet you have many Christian friends who don't celebrate or glorify the dark aspects of the holiday, but they do allow their children to dress up and get a grocery sack full of candy, while using this rare night of open doors as a chance to build relationship with neighbors. These are two different yet viable opinions on Halloween that the Bible doesn't speak to directly.

You feel your conversations with your friends are compelling, and they ask your family to come with them, but you still feel conscience-bound not to participate. It still feels like allowing your kids to trick-or-treat is doing something "wrong." Do you try it just for one year? God's Word would say not to. In Romans 14, Paul says that we need to be "fully convinced in [our] own mind" and that it would be sin to participate or do something that you are not fully convinced of.[3] We're going to quote the New Living Translation here because we think the translation makes this passage easier to understand: "But if you have doubts about whether or not you should eat something, you are sinning if you go ahead and do it. For you are not following your convictions. If you do anything you believe is not right, you are sinning."[4] Follow your conscience, Paul says. Even in areas of freedom or opinion. If you're not personally convinced you have freedom, then don't act on it.

Obey God where you are today, but keep humbly evaluating if you need to. In time, if your conviction changes, then your actions can follow.

What If My Conviction Has Changed, but I Still Feel Weird?

Let's go back to the example of the mom who originally felt her children should not trick-or-treat. Let's say that over the course of the next year, she kept thinking and praying and reading about it every so often, and eventually she came to a biblical conviction that she was free to allow her children to participate as long as they weren't celebrating the underlying spirit of the holiday or glorifying death or darkness. (We, Emily and Laura, aren't taking a stance here; we're just trying to give an example.) Even if she ordered the costumes with confidence and excitement, is on the same page with her husband, and can recall some of the truths she read in Scripture that uphold this new change for her family, she still might feel a little odd that night. That's normal and doesn't necessarily mean that she needs to change her conviction but that her conscience is going to need time to catch up with the change in her beliefs. She can keep humbly evaluating (maybe she does discover that trick-or-treating was worse than she imagined and it wasn't a good influence for her kids, so she's back to the drawing board), but if her conscience was used to thinking something is wrong, that feeling might take time to go away.

---

[3] Romans 14:5.

[4] Romans 14:23 NLT.

OBEY GOD WHERE YOU ARE TODAY.

The same is true when we discover that we're holding on to rules or norms from our family of origin that don't pertain to our current circumstances. For instance, if you grew up in a family where your mom always cooked and did the grocery shopping and your dad never did, it might send your conscience warning bells off when your husband offers to run to the store or take over breakfast every morning of the week. You may know that there is no biblical prohibition on husbands cooking meals or even being the main chef in the household, but it still feels weird or wrong because that's not how your mom and dad did it. You could just be feeling the effects of your personal experience and upbringing, which need to be recalibrated to the marriage God gave *you* over time. It's not necessarily an indication that you should refuse your husband's help.

Always Growing, Never Arriving

Right now, you probably have many areas where your conscience does align with God, but all of us have areas where we might be hypersensitive or in sin that we'll continue to uncover throughout our lives. Chances are, if you've been a believer for a while, you might have noticed how God tends to reveal certain sins or proclivities in batches—not everything all at once. This is a kindness! If he were asking us to work on everything in every facet of life, we would be buried so deep we wouldn't be able to find a way out.

As with many things, once we have a good understanding of God's laws and commands, we'll find that we have freedom where God's Word hasn't given a clear directive. At the end of the day, in these "gray areas," the Lord is often more concerned with who we are and how we go about our decisions than what we specifically decide.

Are we making this decision in faith?
Are we seeking to obey him?
Are we operating with godly wisdom or worldly wisdom?
Are we doing this with words and behaviors that reflect Christ?

You'll never be perfect in this, and that's why redemption is such good news. Christ died for your pride, judgment, guilt, sin, and shame. He redeems you where you misstep in your decisions and feelings and frees you to walk as a new creation. We can have peace and confidence in our decisions, but it doesn't come without doing the work. It's a skill gained over the course of a lifetime, not overnight! Our goal should be to slowly but surely calibrate our consciences to become more and more in line with God's will and Word.

CHAPTER 9

HEART MOTIVATIONS

hen one of our children bursts into a room with tears streaming down their face, the first thing we usually say is, "Oh, honey! What happened?" Maybe you use different mom lingo or a different nickname, but the goal is the same—to uncover the source of their tears. *Who and what hurt them? How did it happen? Was it physical or emotional? What treatment do they need? What will it take to repair and make it better?* In a split second, we go into triage mode, swooping in as a master counselor, detective, and doctor until the tears are wiped and the pain is hopefully relieved.

Yet while we know how to do this symptom checking for our own kids, instinctively drilling down under the obvious problem to find the root cause and solve it, we're not as quick to do this in our own hearts and lives. As moms, when we cry our own tears, well up with anger, eat the whole batch of cookies we just baked, shop for clothes that we don't need late into the night, train for another marathon, and incessantly scroll on social media, we can have a hard time thinking of those as possible symptoms of bigger issues. We might not realize that a bit of curiosity and prayer could go a long way toward discovering that we cry because we have pain from someone who hurt us decades ago or that our anger wells up when we feel defensive about our reputation.

When it comes to gospel thinking and making decisions as Gospel Moms, we're complex creatures. We don't always walk a straight path from biblical principle to clear application—we avoid the path when we think it looks too scary or unsafe, we detour down other paths that seem more appealing, or we link arms with people who are heading in a different direction altogether. Though we just talked a lot about personal conscience and how we have to follow what seems best to us according to our understanding of Scripture in faith, because we live post-Fall, we also have to question our heart motives, dig under the surface, and not automatically trust our gut. And as we make decisions, we ought to play the "mom" role in our own hearts and ask ourselves, *What happened?*

What happened that made you feel like this cosmetic procedure is the only way to manage your fears about aging?

Why do you feel so strongly that you can't ever let your kids listen to secular music?

Where did your fear and bitterness about attending a church small group stem from?

Why is it so important for you to have a toxin-free lifestyle?

The Bible says that our hearts are deceitful, that our ways might seem right to us but that God ultimately is the only one who can see the depths of our hearts and weigh our motives. Remembering that our hearts mislead us at times helps us wisely sift through the various factors in gospel application and decision-making in our unique circumstances. This point in the process is not meant to be discouraging or condemning but helpful, revealing, and ultimately freeing as we understand possible hindrances we have in obedience to God.

Uncover: What Do I Really, Really Want?

Every person was designed to worship. What does it mean to worship? Does it look like bowing down or reciting prayers or even raising your hands as you sing to God? It could, but that's not the only way for someone to fully give themselves to God in worship. Worship is an expression of our commitment to or our adoration of something or someone—it's spending our time, attention, care, words, and precious resources on what we love and value. When we worship, we bring figurative offerings and sacrifices to the altar of something or someone in our lives, and we lay those things down, typically in exchange for something we desire—unconditional love and acceptance, wealth, popularity, happiness, and so on. For Christians, we ought to direct all our worship to the Lord. This is the sum of the first and greatest commandment: You shall love the Lord your God with all your heart, soul, mind, and strength.[1] God is deserving of all that we are and all that we have. Our whole life and breath and thoughts and time and talents and money should be given up in service and gratitude to him. But as fallen humans, that's not often how we direct our worship.

Instead, we tend to struggle with idolatry—worshipping false gods in our lives. Though few people set up actual statues or have figurines in their houses where they might bow or pray, that doesn't mean that we don't have functional idols that we live for. As moms, each of us tends to have pet issues or lifestyles or things we want that are of tremendously high value to us—so high that we're willing to give a ton of time, attention, and money to make them happen. Whether we intend it or notice it doesn't change the fact that those things can become idols in our lives, detracting our worship from the One True God and putting it onto something or someone else.

Someone who idolizes being seen as accomplished or successful might pour an undue amount of time into their work, even to the detriment of their family, their marriage, or their physical health. Someone who idolizes being specially connected to someone talented or famous might pour significant time and money into their child's sports training, competitive leagues, and traveling in hopes that the child will become great and thus

---

[1] Mark 12:30.

GOD IS DESERVING OF ALL THAT WE ARE & ALL THAT WE HAVE.

show everyone else how great their parent is. Few (if any) Christian moms think these things consciously. If we knew that's what we were doing, we'd (hopefully) repent and make changes. But such thinking can creep into our lives unconsciously, and that's also why it's so important for us to soberly and prayerfully evaluate our lives and choices from time to time. Who we *say* we worship (God) might not actually *be* what we worship when we look at our lives and the way we spend our time, attention, and money.

When we have a strong reaction to a situation or decision or we operate in an extreme in some area of our lives or motherhood, these are like little flags of warning. Like the tears of the hurt child who comes into the room, these disproportionate or exorbitant actions or emotions might reveal a need to pause and ask, *What's going on here? What am I worshipping? Is it God or is it something else?*

Uncover: Why Do I Want This So Badly?

Uncovering and tearing down our idols to reorient our worship toward God takes humility, compassion, and curiosity. It takes prayer and the leading of the Spirit, who searches and knows our hearts. It takes being willing to notice where our time and money and energy *actually* go versus where we think they go. It's like the screen-time report that our phones give at the end of each week—it might be hard to look at or something we'd prefer to ignore, but those hours and percentages reveal something about how we're spending our lives and, even more so, what we love, desire, and value deep down.[2]

---

[2] We've found the following list of questions, developed by David Powlison, helpful for believers to uncover their motivations and potential idols: David Powlison, "X Ray Questions by David Powlison," accessed August 23, 2023, http://storage.cloversites.com/crosshaven/documents/xray.pdf.

A NOTE IF YOU'RE DISCOURAGED

As Christian moms who have the Spirit and the flesh, who are redeemed but still living in the Fall and before consummation, our motives (this side of heaven) will never be wholly pure and perfect. We will not be able to fully rid ourselves of other loves or idol worship. We know how hard and frustrating this can be. But we want to pause and encourage you that you don't have to wait until your motives seem totally pure and perfect before you make a decision in faith. Just as it's good to prayerfully evaluate our reasons and motivations, after a time of searching, it's also good to lift our eyes from ourselves and focus them more firmly on God. Beholding him is how we find joy and freedom, and we need to remember the following:

We're not going to solve all of our problems in one go—only the things that God has shown us for now. Try not to let the search for idols paralyze you from moving forward with something that is otherwise good and seems in line with God's will.

It's helpful to examine these things in Christian community so that others can help you sort things out. You might be too hard on yourself in an area that isn't a big deal, or you might be avoiding addressing an area that seems to be obviously out-of-whack to others.

God gave us a spirit not of fear but of love and self-control. He is bigger than our idols, and his grace is bigger than our idolatry. Trust that regular patterns of confession and repentance are doing the good work of sanctification.

Counting the Cost: Strategic Questions for Making Decisions

As we're getting a handle on the things we worship and we start to understand why we do what we do in motherhood, as Gospel Moms navigating "gray areas," we're also going to need to count the cost of our decisions. This is wisdom at play—thinking carefully and strategically about things before we do them, considering the possible risks and rewards, the pros and cons.

When we're busy and have a lot on our plates, it can be easy to just rush from one thing to the next, hastily saying yes or no or going along with the status quo. But believers don't just go along with the status quo or the norm of the culture; they pause and pray. They ask and seek the Lord. Obviously, this would be a pretty clunky thing to stop and do every few minutes of our day—we're not saying you should ask, *Should I get out this set of blocks or that set of books? What are the risks and rewards?* But maybe we should take time every so often to consider what our kids are spending their time on and what toys and activities we make available in the house. Wisdom is applying what we know about God and his Word to the situation we have in front of us, and it's a skill we need in gospel motherhood.

Over the years, as we've thought through topics at Risen Motherhood, we've found several litmus test questions that are helpful for evaluating the risks and rewards of different choices when there isn't a clear right answer.

Is the Cost to Me / Our Family Worth It?

Though the idea of *cost* automatically makes us think of money, money is not the only way to quantify cost. Activities, decisions, lifestyles, and material items can also cost us time and attention. They can drain us emotionally. They can put a strain on our most important relationships, including our relationship with God, wearing down those bonds over time. Different decisions and lifestyle choices can change us and harden our hearts.

When we count the cost of a "gray area" decision, we aren't just thinking of that particular moment—as in whether or not we can physically make it to Saturday morning soccer games ("Sure, we have time on Saturday mornings between nine and noon")—we're also remembering that we'll have to purchase all the gear that goes with it, there might be extra laundry multiple times a week, practices might mean forgoing family dinners together two nights a week, and we might have to then rush everyone off to bed and not spend time on homework or family devotions. We might consider how it's going to impact the younger sibling, who is going to have to sit through these practices and games and/or stay up later than usual. Thinking of these things is trying to count the whole cost before making a decision.

This example is not to be "down" on kids and sports or to say that these costs are never worth it but rather to illustrate that we need to examine things with a desire to see how they truly are, not how we imagine them. And when we soberly count the cost of something in the context of prayer, the Word, our spouse, and our Christian community (where appropriate), when we do move forward and say "yes," we can do so with our eyes wide open to the challenges and risks, ready to try to mitigate them with God's leading and help. For instance, maybe being honest about the way soccer practice is going to impact family dinner times also encourages you and your husband to get more creative about other times to have together, or maybe you move family devotion time to breakfast.

Counting the cost isn't limited to kids' activities. We can count the cost of being or not being involved in a Bible study through church. We can count the cost of making regular relational investments with our spouse over and against the cost of not doing so. We can count the cost of going back to school and getting another degree or taking on a major work project. We can count the cost of our time spent looking at our phone versus looking up at our children.

Though we're not God and we're not going to be able to fully consider all the angles and things that might come up (and sometimes this is trial and error), we don't have to be afraid of the fact that our choices have costs and consequences—just curious and aware about them.

BEHOLDING GOD IS HOW WE FIND JOY & FREEDOM.

How Does This Align with Our Circumstances and Values?

Just as we explored in discussing unique circumstances (chapter 7), we can remember that every family has a unique makeup and unique God-given areas of emphasis. When we're considering a decision, we might look back to a family mission statement or consider a special annual planning session that we did with our husband and how this decision aligns with those aims.

Before we spend time and money on something, we have to consider how it fits into our kingdom mission as a woman, a wife, a mom, and as a family unit as a part of the church, both locally and globally. Sometimes we see other people doing things that look interesting or amazing, and we adopt those goals for ourselves, only to realize later (if we're being honest) that those things don't fit the lives and circumstances that God has given us. This is where it's helpful to ask questions about our motivations and try to uncover why we want to do something—is it because we really think this aligns with the way God is leading us in our lives, or is it because we feel pressure from others or we're seeking to lay hold of something we idolize?

How Permanent Is This Decision?

Some decisions are easy to change—you can leave the house and head to a pizza place and then, along the way, decide to take a different exit and grab fried chicken for dinner instead. One night you might decide to forgo a full night's sleep to stay up and finish a home organization project, but the next day you decide to go to bed early to prioritize rest. These types of decisions take thought, but because they are so easy to pivot from, they aren't usually the ones we wrestle with the most. If the Spirit leads you differently, you can change quickly.

Some decisions come with a higher level of commitment, and though they can be changed, it might mean letting someone down or breaking your word. These decisions take more time, thought, and special evaluation—maybe even every few months. Technically, you can unenroll your kids from the school you've selected midyear if something isn't going well, and that might be okay and how God leads you, but you wouldn't want to make that decision hastily. The same might be true for work or a volunteer commitment.

And some decisions are nearly permanent (in this life). Though there are always things we can do to repent and pivot and seek redemption and restoration, we want to proceed with these types of decisions with self-control and caution. For instance, deciding who we marry, or guarding our tongue in heated moments before we utter harmful words that can't be unsaid, or having surgeries that might alter our body or the course of a child's life. We don't need to live in fear of these decisions, but if possible, the level of permanency of a decision should correlate with the level of time, care, consideration, and attention we give it before we move forward.

Can I Be Transparent About This Decision?

Just like we talked about in discussing the personal conscience (chapter 8), sometimes things don't sit well with us not because they are wrong but because of the way we've been wired through our upbringing or culture. We're always seeking to further align our conscience with the Holy Spirit and God's Word. But sometimes, we get a bad feeling about something or want to hide it from others because deep down, in some way, we know or think it's wrong. Again, this is why it's so important to look under the surface of actions and choices to see what's really going on—why we are giving up so much to have something, or why we are isolating ourselves from Christian community, or what's causing us to not be transparent with safe people in our lives. What about this decision or lifestyle choice makes it something that I want or need to keep under wraps? Maybe it's because everyone around you is living in an unbiblical way, and you're being faithful, but you're worried what they'll think of you. Or maybe it's because the choices you're making are veering away from God's Word, and you don't want to have to reckon with that reality.

There's no biblical precedent that we need to share everything we do with everyone, but we are accountable to some people who should have a healthy ability to look into our lives and offer encouragement or even a gentle rebuke. Maybe you have a growing collection of high-end designer handbags, but you feel that you can't bring them to certain events or to a church gathering. That's not to say owning the handbags is wrong, but your discomfort is a good prompt to pause and ask, "Why?" *Why do I feel bad about this in some situations?* Maybe you start a new diet every three months, and though your husband knows, you never talk about it with any of your friends from your church small group. Deep down you long to have a culturally praised body type, but you also have this nagging feeling that maybe you're spending too much time, money, or energy on this, all for the sake of your own physical appearance. That's not to say focusing on nutrition, a healthy diet, or exercise is wrong, but maybe those feelings are a sign that you should stop and ask, "Why?" *Why do I feel like this needs to be done in secret?*

The aim of these questions isn't to prompt guilt or condemnation or to size yourself up. The aim is to be able to walk in freedom, being able to live for God's glory without fear, guilt, or shame. There may be good answers to why you don't share everything you do with others. (Maybe keeping the handbags at home is a way to show modesty in certain situations, or maybe not sharing your diet is a way to love your sisters at church who struggle with disordered eating.) Keep processing and praying and asking questions and having those helpful conversations with believing friends until you are at peace with what God's Word says and how you're applying it in your life.

Trust the Process

There are so many things in life that start out looking and seeming a little odd or weird, but in the end, they turn out well. At the beginning of the haircut, it might have seemed like the stylist was cutting too much off or asking us to turn our head in a strange direction, but she told us to "trust the process," and by the end, it (hopefully) looked great. Or maybe you were getting your makeup done for a special event and the blush started out looking too bright, but when the whole look came together in pictures, it looked amazing. "Trust the process" is a way of saying that you can't judge the end result too soon or give up if it's not looking exactly like you imagined. In fact, giving up too soon is a sure way to be totally frustrated and disappointed.

The same is often true as we evaluate decisions and seek to walk by the Spirit as a Gospel Mom. We're fallen sinners, saved by grace, hopefully growing in holiness but experiencing a lot of setbacks and missteps along the way. We're complex women full of skills and hurts and questions and hesitations. We have lives and seasons that are constantly changing, making it hard to predict what's next. All of these factors can make it feel like all of this motivation uncovering and question asking is hopeless. But…trust the process!

CHAPTER 10

BUT WHAT DO WE DO ABOUT ALL THE OTHER MOMS?

O n paper, we (Emily and Laura) are pretty similar moms. We're the same age, race, religion, and socioeconomic status. We're both married with school-age kids, we live in the same subculture, and we each have a child with disabilities. We even live almost within the same square mile! But that doesn't mean we're identical moms who do everything exactly the same. In fact, you'd find there are some big differences in how we raise our kids and structure our days. In particular, when we were moms to young children, making many of our mothering decisions for the very first time, we had moments where we didn't always understand why the other was making the choices she made. And in some ways, because we were so similar, it was almost harder to understand when one of us deviated from what we thought was the "best" or "right" choice.

Even as moms who preached the gospel to ourselves consistently and had a growing understanding of what it meant to apply biblical wisdom and respect others' and our own personal conscience, it took time to get comfortable with the reality that God would lead both of us individually and specifically in our own motherhood journey. A different choice didn't mean we should make ourselves the judge who determined if the other mom was "outside God's will" or failing to be faithful. It also didn't always mean that we needed to question our own choices, as if being different were in and of itself a red flag that one of us was doing something wrong. Avoiding the extremes of judgment and self-doubt is easier said than done!

We're willing to bet a date night out that you've faced this too. You've struggled to understand another mom's choice or felt sidelined when your closest mom pal decided to do something that felt contrary to your own decisions. It doesn't matter if it's something small like not putting up the child safety locks you recommended or giving her child a later curfew, or something big like selecting a different type of schooling than you did or not taking your cell phone advice. We've all felt the ground shake when we realize we're alone in our choice, and this doesn't just happen with our friends. It happens in an even greater magnitude when you overlap with other moms who are in different stages of life than you or have vastly different cultural contexts. And we haven't even discussed the impacts of the internet and the staunch camps that exist to pressure you and your friends into a certain way of living.

Even as we make decisions and begin to walk in freedom within our own circumstances, we still doubt and still question: *I thought I was making the right choice, but was I really? I was confident in my decision, but should I change?* Or maybe in some situations, it's *What should I do if I do believe a mom is making a wrong choice in her life? What do I tell her, and what do I hold back?*

Remember, the thing about being a Gospel Mom is that it's rooted in God and his Word and (have you heard us say this enough yet?) not a specific lifestyle or parenting choice. That means we are going to apply aspects of his design differently and still be faithful, and this is a beautiful thing! But we admit, sometimes it's hard to see the beauty. We just see doubt, judgment, and questions. So how do we adhere to our convictions and live in unity with other moms? Thankfully, the Bible addresses this.

Honoring God in Differences

Unity wasn't and isn't just a lesson that Christian moms need to hear; it's one for all believers. When the apostle Paul was spreading the gospel to Gentiles and going around to different churches, he came up against a multitude of questions and concerns. How were all of these different people—from different cultures, with different native languages and understandings of what it meant to honor God through their practices and traditions—going to live together in unity? How were they going to know what was right and wrong, and what if those things looked different from other believers in their local church or community?

In 1 Corinthians 10:23-33, the Lord gave Paul an incredible word of wisdom for those believers in the early church that helps us wisely seek wisdom today:

> "All things are lawful," but not all things are helpful. "All things are lawful," but not all things build up. Let no one seek his own good, but the good of his neighbor. Eat whatever is sold in the meat market without raising any question on the ground of conscience. For "the earth is the Lord's, and the fullness thereof." If one of the unbelievers invites you to dinner and you are disposed to go, eat whatever is set before you without raising any question on the ground of conscience. But if someone says to you, "This has been offered in sacrifice," then do not eat it, for the sake of the one who informed you, and for the sake of conscience—I do not mean your conscience, but his. For why should my liberty be determined by someone else's conscience? If I partake with thankfulness, why am I denounced because of that for which I give thanks? So, whether you eat or drink, or whatever you do, do all to the glory of God. Give no offense to Jews or to Greeks or to the church of God, just as I try to please everyone in everything I do, not seeking my own advantage, but that of many, that they may be saved.

In the context of his letter to the church of Corinth, we see Paul addressing some of the idolatry and division that the church experienced as they made different choices about whether or not to eat meat that had been sacrificed to idols. Though we don't have much context for this debate in our modern faith, we are familiar with lots of other debates that Christian moms have— like whether or not you can have income-producing work outside of the home (and if so, how much), whether or not you ought to homeschool or pursue other school options, what you feed your kids, or how clean, natural, low-tech, holistic, and toxin-free your lifestyle is, just to name a few. What if we thought about what Paul was saying and applied it to some of the most controversial, identity-shaping questions of modern Christian motherhood?

Blood pressure might start to rise.

But instead of getting us all worked up, this actually should be a way for us to all calm down.

Look at the summation of what Paul said in this incredible line: "Whatever you do, do all to the glory of God."[1] This is one of those Bible verses that's plastered on mugs, journals, and T-shirts. It's one some of us are so familiar with that our eyes glaze over and we nod along, "Yeah, yeah, God's glory. I know." But do we really know? Do we really get what that means for us as moms?

Let's unpack a few key points from these verses together, because our understanding of this concept in our lives as Gospel Moms will change so much of how we feel about other moms' choices and how we engage with them. A lot of this will bring in things we discussed in the personal conscience and heart motivation chapters (see, it really does all come together!), and we'll try to point that out where we can.

> *"All things are lawful," but not all things are helpful.*
> *"All things are lawful," but not all things build up.*[2]

Because our sins are fully paid for by the blood of Christ and are as far

---

[1] 1 Corinthians 10:31.

[2] 1 Corinthians 10:23.

away from us as the east is from the west, and because we're no longer being judged under the law as the Israelites were but the law was fulfilled by Christ and we're under grace, we don't think and make decisions with fear. This passage talks about meat and whether or not it had been sacrificed to an idol. Even though that animal had been used for something wrong (ritual sacrifice to a false god), it was made by and belongs to the Lord, and—according to Paul—a believer could technically eat it, give thanks to God, and not violate any of God's laws.

But there's a big and important caveat here: just because the recipients of Paul's letters *could* do something didn't mean they *should*. And the same is true for us today. As Gospel Moms, we have tremendous freedom to live in different ways—to feed our kids different foods, live in different areas, use different types of laundry detergent, play different styles of music, spend our time and our days in different ways, and school our children differently. We can have different lives and interests, but we have to realize that not all things build up the church and point others to Christ. As Gospel Moms, we ought to consider not just how our decisions impact us but how they impact and communicate the gospel to others, especially if and where our lives intersect.

We aren't a family on an island; we live in the midst of other moms also trying to raise their kids in the Lord! Though we get to make our own decisions according to how the Lord leads us (and that's not the sole determining factor in our decisions), we can still show deference and refuse to cast guilt and fear on moms around us. This might be made clearer with the next point Paul makes.

Let no one seek his own good, but the good of his neighbor.[3]

As Gospel Moms, we're not just seeking to have our own way; we're seeking to love one another in Christ. For example, you are free to drink a glass of wine with dinner, and maybe for you, doing so is not a temptation

---

[3] 1 Corinthians 10:24.

toward sin or a problem. In fact, maybe you delight in the flavor profiles and the art of winemaking, thinking of biblical parallels and giving thanks to God. But if you have a bunch of moms over, it would be good to consider how that might impact them. What does it communicate about what you value? Are there any moms there who do struggle with wise alcohol consumption, so offering it to them might tempt them to stumble? Does it build them up in the Lord to have a line of wine bottles uncorked and ready to drink? It could feel like a big sacrifice to lay that down, but an important one if it's for the sake of loving your neighbor. The main question here is this: Though you have freedoms, how do you seek the good of others?[4] Romans 14:13 says, "Therefore let us not pass judgment on one another any longer, but rather decide never to put a stumbling block or hindrance in the way of a brother."

A more tender example might be the way you approach situations and conversations with a friend who has recently had a miscarriage. You might have been so excited to talk with her about the ways you're preparing for childbirth and have conversations about your worries and anxieties. But as you're interacting with her, you might lay aside some of your own desires and goals and instead choose to be more cautious about your words and speak in a way that recognizes she's hurting. It doesn't necessarily mean you totally avoid the topic or never acknowledge your own cares and concerns, but you seek her good and care for her heart, even if it steers the conversation differently.

> *Give no offense…I try to please everyone in everything I do, not seeking my own advantage, but that of many, that they may be saved.*[5]

In all of this, Paul had a specific aim—not that he would get everything he wanted or live in a way that was most comfortable for him, but that he

---

[4] See appendix B for more details on how to think through areas of Christian freedom, personal conscience, and loving others.

[5] 1 Corinthians 10:32-33.

SEEK
THE GOOD
OF THOSE
AROUND YOU,
AND CARE
FOR THEIR
HEARTS.

would live in such a way that contributed to the spread of the gospel and the salvation of many. Many of us go about our days wondering what would be the easiest thing to do or even what would be the most advantageous for our career, reputation, social media feed, bank account, and family. But we give little thought to how we can try to please and serve others outside of our family and outside of ourselves. Few of us ponder what it looks like to make choices in ways that don't just consider ourselves but consider the impact on the church, our Christian witness, or even those who don't yet believe in our community.

In part 1, "The Framework," we talked about how important it is to remember that as Christian moms, we're swept up into a greater story and we have a bigger purpose than what we can see—to be part of God's redemptive work in his kingdom until Christ returns. The story isn't about us, and life isn't about us having our version of the "perfect life" or a "perfect motherhood." It's about us seeing how we fit into the bigger picture and living our lives in such a way that evangelism and the Great Commission stay at the forefront of our minds.

> *So, whether you eat or drink, or whatever you do, do all to the glory of God.*[6]

With all these things in mind, we finally get to the coffee-mug Bible verse with a better understanding of what it truly means. Whatever we do—as we make daily decisions in the gray areas of life, as we seek to be Gospel Moms and apply biblical principles by the Spirit's guidance—we want to do it all to the glory of God.

What does it mean to do something to God's glory? Let's consider a few ways.

We think, act, speak, and live in ways that show others the character and ways of God. He gets the glory (esteem, attention, and honor) when people

---

[6] 1 Corinthians 10:31.

leave our presence or our homes both having seen us live in obedience to God and also feeling loved, seen, and provided for in ways that are beyond what a mere human could do. This might mean:

- We have self-control when a child throws a tantrum or goes into an emotional wave, parenting with compassion, love, and truth.

- We consider, have compassion for, use charity toward, and are genuinely curious about other moms' choices when we don't understand, instead of instantly assuming that because she does something different from us, she must be doing something wrong.

- We prioritize asking deeper, heart-level questions of a mom friend, showing we really care instead of just sharing our own concerns or "swapping information" about other moms in the neighborhood.

- We look for opportunities to give time and attention to others who are struggling, hurting, or not socially advantageous to us. We reserve time in our days to text a grieving friend, take a meal to a new mom, or have a conversation with someone who needs a friend.

- Even in our severely limited or busy seasons, we can pray for others and do our best to be present with the people who we do come in contact with.

We praise God for who he is and the work he's done in our lives and share that with others, giving credit to him alone. Just as we rave about a good restaurant to our closest friends, sharing every detail of our favorite dish and encouraging them to go and try it, as Gospel Moms, we ought to be quick to acknowledge and share joyfully about the grace and provision of God in our lives. This might mean:

- We serve our kids fast food that night, praying and giving thanks to God for his provision of both the bread that our bodies need and Christ, the bread of life.

- We don't openly or slyly take credit for the way we spend our time or money but try to serve under the radar and share about how God has given to us when we're asked about the reason for our generosity.

- We invite others to study the Bible or talk about Jesus with us.

- We speak honestly about who God is and how he's working in our lives, even when we're around unbelievers.

We live in such a way that shows God is at the center of our attention and worship. This shows his worthiness, preeminence, and majesty because our lives only orbit around what's most important and central. This might mean:

- We evaluate our family schedule to see if we're orienting our lives around sports or entertainment versus Christ and the church.

- We take inventory of our material possessions and engagements to see if we're storing up treasures for ourselves on earth versus in heaven.

- We evaluate our own personal time spent on social media apps to see if we're giving attention to the right people and information.

- We commit to a daily time with the Lord to fix our eyes on him and keep him as the main priority in our lives.

This might feel abstract, but that's simply because we have such a strong desire for hacks, silver bullets, five-step plans, and self-help overhauls. Having things broken down into steps and tips is really helpful, and there is a time and place for that even in our spiritual learning, but giving glory to God in all things takes faith.

Maybe a scenario will help. Let's take a look at two moms, Lucy and Sarah, who go to the same church and are great friends, but they handle health and medicine in different ways. Now, there might be multiple heart issues going on here, but for the sake of this example, we're going to assume that we're not dealing with lots of pride and idolatry.

Lucy:

Lucy and her husband have a three-year-old son and a one-year-old daughter. After a nasty cold virus hits the whole house, Lucy's daughter starts waking up from naps crying. Lucy gives her infant over-the-counter medicine for the pain she seems to be in and waits it out. A day or so later, Lucy's daughter spiked a fever and is now waking up on and off throughout the night. Lucy continues to give her pain medication and takes her daughter to the doctor the next day. The doctor tells her that an ear appears to be infected and prescribes her an antibiotic. Lucy goes home, picks up the prescription, and thanks God for the availability of medicine. Her daughter seems happy and is back to normal within 24 hours. Lucy is happy she took action.

Sarah:

Sarah and her husband have twin two-year-old sons. After a nasty cold virus hits the whole house, both of Sarah's sons start waking up at night with low fevers, crying on and off in pain. Instead of heading to the doctor, Sarah decides to use some at-home medicinal techniques. She thanks God for the availability of naturopathic medicines and other natural remedies she learned about from her grandmother, her friends, and even someone she follows online. She monitors her sons closely, comforting them over the course of several days. Eventually, her sons start feeling better. Sarah is glad she didn't take them to the doctor and is glad she didn't have to use antibiotics.

Analysis:

Although you might have strong opinions or intense feelings of conscience about this, we don't think Scripture gives clear direction about what types of medicine or health treatments are most holy or godly. Every culture, people group, and age does it a little differently. Someone in China is likely going to medically treat their child differently from someone in Texas. This is a gray area. It's a matter of conscience. Lucy and Sarah are two moms who acted according to their personal consciences, doing what they thought was best in a desire to honor God and love their children. They had general "freedom in Christ" to use either type of medical treatment, but personally, they were bound to their consciences.

Lucy's conscience had no problem with giving pain medicine, seeing the doctor, and using the prescribed antibiotics. She saw this as a way to trust God in faith and love her daughter well. It would have violated her conscience to stay home from the doctor when she "knew" there was a way to help her that she failed to utilize. Sarah's conscience would have been violated by using medication and sending her sons to the doctor so quickly. For her, acting in faith and loving her children meant praying and utilizing the tools at her disposal at home first.

Remember, Sarah and Lucy have a lot in common. They're both moms to young children, live in the same town, and go to the same church. They can live together in unity around the gospel and the whole Word of God only as long as they aren't trying to make the other person "convert" to their way. This is how moms live out Paul's teaching—*whatever you do, do all to the glory of God.* They're comfortable with differences. This might mean that when Lucy sees that Sarah's boys are sick, she's not constantly asking, "When are you going to get them on antibiotics?!" making her feel like she's doing something terrible. And conversely, Sarah isn't giving Lucy a condescending look every time she hears that Lucy's daughter is on antibiotics for an ear infection. There might be room for them to learn from each other at various points in their relationship, but it shouldn't be an ongoing source of contention, division, and disunity in their relationship. They can see that the other mom is free to make her choices and still be a loving mother who is following the Lord's leading.

As a Gospel Mom, you're seeking to humbly align your heart and actions with the Lord as you love those around you, not just make outwardly "good" choices with a heart of pride and self-sufficiency. Similarly, in gray-area decisions, it's important to care about the motives and heart posture of another mom and not just the choice she's making. This perspective puts God, his ways, and our hearts at the center of our focus, not just our choices and behaviors.

When You're Not the Right Fit

Even as we're careful to love other moms well in gray areas, there are going to be times when we so deeply feel something is right and obedient to God that it feels shocking or discouraging to us when other moms view things differently. We may even feel that they are sinning against their families. While you should always seek to understand and feel like you can speak truth to her and ask questions, also know that believers are going to disagree about things. This is why we need a theology of unity, and what we wrote about in chapter 8 is a good place to start.

Sometimes, we need a reminder that we don't have to be best friends with everyone. If there is a mom who you really don't align with on issues of personal conscience, and you can't see eye to eye or get to a point where you understand or respect where her conscience lies, you don't have to feel pressure to spend a lot of time with her. Perhaps her conscience is so firm on certain topics that she causes feelings of anxiety or fear each time you engage with her. Conversely, maybe you recognize that while you're trying to be sensitive, you can't censor your lifestyle from her completely to honor her boundaries. In these cases, you can still show her love and kindness when you interact with her and ensure that you speak about her with integrity and truth, but you don't have to be close friends with her if it is particularly challenging to maintain a relationship. If she sincerely follows Christ, trust that the Spirit is at work in her life and her family just as he is in yours.

What a Wonderful World It Could Be

We quoted the apostle Paul a lot in this chapter. He converted to Christianity out of being a Pharisee, which meant he had a jumble of things he needed to sort through in order to discern what was truly required of him as a believer and what were additional Jewish laws. He probably had all sorts of things mixed up about what was "good" and "bad" or "right" and "wrong." God was faithful and clearly helped him recalibrate after his conversion. In 1 Corinthians 9, just before the passage we used for this chapter, he talks of how he was "so free" he was able to be whatever he needed to be—not so that he could do anything he wanted but so "that by all means [he] might save some."[7] He says, "I do it all for the sake of the gospel, that I may share with them in its blessings."[8]

Can you imagine what our world would look like if this was the posture we took as moms? If we said along with Paul, "For though I am free from all, I have made myself a servant to all, that I might win more of them"?[9] This is how we build bridges between moms who are different from us. It's how homeschool, public school, and private school moms become friends. It's how the working mom and the stay-at-home mom support each other. It's how the traditional medical mom and the all-natural mom swap knowledge and skills.

---

[7] 1 Corinthians 9:22.

[8] 1 Corinthians 9:23.

[9] 1 Corinthians 9:19.

As Gospel Moms, it's about knowing not just *what to do* but *who to be*. It's about being willing to trust God to lead and guide us as we learn about him, rest in him, and go to him for wisdom. We give God glory precisely because we aren't able to strong-arm our way into an awesome life by doing a bunch of good things; instead, we walk humbly by faith as he does his transforming work in our hearts.

CONCLUSION

GOSPEL MOM

CHAPTER 11

WHAT KIND
OF MOMS?

Remember the scene from the beginning of the book? The mom who watched her daughter change and grow from a pajama-clad toddler to a young woman going off to college? Imagine that same mom now with gray hair and soft eyes, sitting in a rocking chair. She has watched her daughter grow and change through the years, rejoicing when she got married and created a home of her own, and weeping tears of joy when she had her own child. Now the mom's mottled hands smooth the blanket that holds her first great-granddaughter.

The mom knows she was not perfect in this life, but she strove to be a Gospel Mom and was as faithful as she could be with what she knew of Scripture, her faith, and her life circumstances in each season. Over the years, she's seen God continue to shape and refine her character in peace, patience, kindness, self-control, and more. She can't believe God's kindness—that he used the many small, mundane deposits she made in her children's lives to lead them to know Christ for themselves. She prays quietly over this new gift of life. She smiles as she thinks of the incredible impacts of the gospel as it is shared from generation to generation. She prays that every mom will love Christ and center their life around the good news that his life, death, and resurrection bring—and that they will know the peace, joy, and freedom

God so longs to provide for them. She knows it is not long now until she meets her Savior. While she is grateful for every moment she still has with those she loves, she can't wait to bow before the God who has walked so closely with her in this earthly life.

By now, you're at the end of this book, and we've thrown a lot of information at you. But hopefully, things are beginning to crystallize for you as you catch a vision of what it looks like to truly believe that the gospel changes everything and that you really can live as a Gospel Mom. As we mentioned in the first chapter, the gospel is so simple and beautiful that in many ways, it's not complicated—*Just live by the Word of God and follow him in faith!*—yet we also know that when the rubber meets the road, living the gospel can feel vague and complex. We pray that this book has provided you with help and hope where Christian motherhood feels confusing or murky. It's designed to serve as one of many great ways to understand God's call for not just what to do but *who to be.*

To do that, we've looked at the following:

The framework of the gospel narrative: Creation, Fall, Redemption, and Consummation. While Scripture can feel ancient and disconnected from our modern lives as moms, if we know where and how to look, it really does speak to everything we face.

The practices that scaffold the life of a Gospel Mom. Spiritual disciplines and habits give our lives stable practices that shape us to be more like Christ.

The thinking that pulls everything together, particularly when we get to gray areas of Christian motherhood. Your unique circumstances, personal conscience, and heart motivations matter as you make decisions to the glory of God.

These are a lot of components to keep in mind, but the exciting thing is that they leave a lot of room for freedom! Not the kind of freedom that has no boundaries, but the kind of freedom that gives us pleasant and safe boundaries of God's Word, a new heart, God-aligned desires, and the power and ability to live more and more like him.

But we also know how easy it can be to see gospel motherhood as just another formula to reach "good mom" status. Over our years of running the ministry of Risen Motherhood, we've even found ourselves falling into this trap, treating the gospel framework as a handbook or model and assuming it will spit out the right answer to give us instant clarity and peace every time. We've found ourselves joking that we could apply the gospel to potato chips if we needed to (which is not really a joke; we actually could), but sometimes, if we're not paying attention, we become more caught up in solving the puzzle than loving and becoming like Christ. We're still tempted to think that if we can just focus our gospel lens right, then we'll be super-Christian moms. But here's the danger: While putting effort into biblical motherhood is good and aids in our sanctification, we can err if we attempt to earn God's favor and acceptance by mastering this method. We don't seek our security and "goodness" in a system or Christian stereotype; we find all of our security and goodness in Christ himself.

As you read this book, there might have been times it felt confusing, dry, or complex. Or perhaps you understood it and felt inspired in the moment but then felt befuddled when it came to applying it to a real situation in your own life. Or maybe you immediately applied these skills, and you applied them well, but you still felt doubts or concerns tying you up and wondered what you did wrong. It feels like two steps forward, one step back. Oh sister, we get this! But hey, one step is still progress! Please don't let this deter you from continuing to grow as a Gospel Mom. This is utterly normal, and you're not alone.

Measuring gospel growth isn't the same as measuring progress in other areas of our lives. We are so trained to look at traditional measures of success or "goodness" in our lives—numbers, trips, projects, sales, check marks, lists, signatures. We like marks of visible success. These things can be helpful in some contexts, but being a Christian means that we don't have a full view of the results of our work yet, and for now the yield can feel unimpressive. It requires faith that God is working even when we can't see it or observe measurable outputs. As God teaches and trains us, he shapes us like a sculptor. Sometimes he uses a file, sometimes a deep chisel. More often than not, the changes occur little by little, sometimes in such small ways we hardly even notice. There can be progress and then regress—steps forward and then back. Either way, our job is to be faithful to do the work of knowing and applying the gospel and to trust the Lord to do the rest, even if it's not on our timeline.

Success as a Gospel Mom isn't about how impressive or measurable the output is, but it's about the obedience and faith of the input. God uses small, foolish things to do massive kingdom-changing work, and sometimes the fruit God wants to grow takes generations.

Perks of Being a Gospel Mom

As you've learned by now, God doesn't offer a precise formula for our lives, but he does offer direction through his Word, the help of the Holy Spirit working in our hearts, and boundless grace, mercy, love, and peace along the way. Of course, the most important and life-changing thing you get when you believe the gospel is salvation in Christ. You get to personally know and be in the presence of the God of the universe, have his Spirit inside you, and live with him now and through eternity. This is the greatest gift of all!

But as you close the last pages of this book, we can't let you go without exploring some of the other incredible things we receive. Remember, a Gospel Mom does the following:

Gains a new heart and a new nature with Christ's righteousness. You do good not to earn anything but because good has been done for you and you know you are capable of following and obeying God's commands.

GOD IS WORKING EVEN WHEN WE CAN'T SEE IT. OUR JOB IS TO BE FAITHFUL.

Knows her mission and purpose. No matter your earthly accolades, you live a life sold out for Christ, displaying his goodness to the world around you and sharing the reason for the hope that you have.

Lives free from the punishment of sin yet still wrestles with its power. You won't be perfect, and you will struggle with this tension of a sin nature until you reach heaven's shores. You know God is in the business of redemption—nothing is too far gone or too bad for him to redeem.

Understands the realities of a broken earth and the hardship of life east of Eden. You know suffering and sorrow will be constant companions throughout your days on earth, and you don't expect life to always be easy.

Lives free from mom guilt. Because there is no condemnation for those who are in Christ and your sins are fully paid for, you don't have to suffer under the suffocating weight of mom guilt. If you're struggling, you can dig under the surface and uncover whether you're experiencing true conviction from the Holy Spirit or condemnation as you fail to meet your own or your culture's ideals.

Rejoices because nothing can separate her from the love of God. When you fail, you can tell God, repent, and keep trusting him. He isn't mad at you or disappointed. He loves you more than you can ever imagine. You know God promises to help you, through the guidance of his Word and his Spirit and other people around you.

Recognizes the battle is against the world, the flesh, and the devil—not other moms. You know the battle isn't really about methods, ideas, or opinions on motherhood but instead against the spiritual forces of evil. You know who the true enemy is, and you stand your ground.

Walks in freedom from fear. While you know there are many things you could fear in this life, ultimately you only fear the Lord and believe that he is in control of all things. You rest secure that it's not up to you to control every variable or protect from all harm.

Trusts God to continue to grow and change her. You know you are sealed with the promise of the Holy Spirit who is living and active inside of you, growing you day by day into the likeness of Christ.

Sets her sight on eternity and the glory that awaits. You don't live for the immediate rewards of today in your marriage or kids, your bank account, or your circumstances. Your gaze is fixed on the person and work of Christ and what matters for eternity. You live with hope and a future.

These are the good news principles of the gospel that will see you through to the end. If you take nothing else from this book, we pray you latch on to these truths with a white-knuckle grip. Like the mom in our story who has walked with the Lord day by day, year by year, and decade by decade, believe in the hope of Christ. Trust that his heart is kind, good, and benevolent toward you. Be united with Jesus and his goodness as you rest in the transcendent and divine truths of the gospel that will carry you all the way to the holy gates of heaven.

We won't do motherhood perfectly, but thankfully, we don't have to.

What kind of moms are we going to be? Gospel Moms.

APPENDIXES

GOSPEL-THINKING QUESTIONS

Below you'll find a compilation of questions to help you process any situation in motherhood through the framework of the gospel. These aren't meant to be formulaic, but we do hope they will prompt time with Scripture, prayer, and good conversations with godly mentors as you seek to understand aspects of your motherhood. These questions are intentionally ambiguous so you can apply them to a wide variety of situations in motherhood.

Creation

1. How did God originally intend or design this to be?

2. How would it function without sin and brokenness?

3. How does it reflect the beauty of who God is?

4. Where does Scripture address this topic and the ways God has designed it to flourish?

5. What principles, standards, or truths have remained for all people for all of time?

Fall

1. How have sin and brokenness caused a divergence from God's design in this situation or area of life?

2. How has sin infiltrated my thoughts, words, or actions, and how is it keeping me from living according to God's good plan?

3. Am I sinning by commission (doing something I shouldn't) or omission (not doing something I should)?

4. What influences am I applying from the culture around me?

5. Where does Scripture address this topic and how it deviates from God's plan because of sin? What are the consequences?

6. In what ways am I trying to redeem myself or fix the situation on my own by changing my outside circumstances?

7. What do I need to repent of in this situation?

Redemption

1. How can I look to Christ's example while he was on earth as a model on this topic?

2. Where does Scripture show how Christ has redeemed this topic?

3. After thinking on creation and the Fall, in what areas do I see myself allowing lingering feelings of guilt and shame that God has not placed on me? In what areas is my guilt due to sin that I need to repent for?

4. Am I placing any unnecessary cultural or personal rules or laws on myself that God hasn't mandated?

5. How does knowing I am already eternally called "good" before God because of Christ free me to "do good" in this situation through the power of the Holy Spirit?

6. How can I steward this situation or relationship in a way that honors God and is a means of evangelism or discipleship?

Consummation

1. How does the assurance of future hope in eternity change my perspective and give me a purpose and a mission today?

2. How can I see that God is working for my greatest good in this situation, knowing he is sovereign and I am part of the greater story he is writing?

3. Someday Christ will perfectly administer all justice and make all things right. How can that give me comfort today?

4. In what ways can I see that I am growing newer even while my body grows older?

5. If I have Jesus, what do I have to lose in this life?

6. What verses, songs, and truths can I repeat to anchor my hope in Christ through my ever-changing circumstances?

Other

1. If I am married, what does my husband think?

2. What advice or insight have people from my local church or wise friends offered?

3. What is the Lord moving in my heart through reflections after time in prayer?

PERSONAL CONSCIENCE AND LOVING OTHER MOMS

A s Christian moms, we're going to be in situations where we've worked through our own conscience issues and have peace and freedom, but our position might be in opposition to that of a good friend who landed in a totally different spot. Fortunately, the Bible provides clear guidance for such a situation, and in Romans 14, Paul talks about how to think about conscience in the context of a relationship. Key to his teaching is the idea of the *strong conscience*. A "strong" conscience means you have a strong understanding of what is biblically right and wrong and where Christian freedoms lie. It's so "strong" that it is tolerant of different understandings in those areas and lives free from guilt. A strong conscience is a great thing! And it also bears certain responsibilities.

Respect Where Others' Consciences Are Bound

First, you're not to put someone who has a weaker conscience in a position where they have to violate their conscience. This means that sometimes you might feel freedom in an area, but you'll decide to do something (or not do something) even though you know you have freedom. For example, let's say you let your children play certain video games. Yet you know your neighbor believes those video games are not age-appropriate for her children and doesn't allow them. You can honor her choices, even in an area where you feel unbound, by not allowing the video game console to come out when her children are over.

Romans 14:13 says, "Therefore let us not pass judgment on one another any longer, but rather decide never to put a stumbling block or hindrance in the way of a brother." In order to live in unity with our sisters in Christ, we should never try to manipulate or violate an area where their conscience is bound.

Don't Flaunt Your Freedoms

Second, God never wants us to use our strong conscience, or "freedom in Christ," to be unloving. We often see this from seasoned mothers. As children get older, moms typically become more comfortable in their role, and it can be easy to look at new mothers and think they're being overly cautious or tied up in knots over unimportant things. While seasoned moms might be more discerning about what's truly right and wrong and what's simply a matter of preference, it doesn't give them an excuse to flaunt their own areas of freedom of conscience.

In Romans 14:1, Paul writes, "As for the one who is weak in faith, welcome him, but not to quarrel over opinions." A mom with a stronger conscience might think it's fine to have a variety of extracurricular activities in her kid's life during different seasons, but a mom with a weaker conscience might believe that extracurricular activities are dangerous to the healthy development of family culture. One mom might not bat an eye at a kiddo's mention of a tummy ache, but another mom might take that as grounds to cancel a playdate and not understand why others wouldn't do the same. It doesn't mean that the mom with a stronger conscience doesn't have an opinion, nor does it mean that we don't need to use or share wisdom and discernment as we make choices. Rather, a strong conscience means that we recognize areas of Christian freedom, trusting God to lead each mom individually in her unique circumstances.

Trust God to Lead Each Mom

Relationships with other moms are tough, especially when you have different ideas about what's right and wrong based on your personal conscience. But as moms, we can be gentle and compassionate about where others are with their own conscience, trusting that the Holy Spirit is the only one who causes true conviction and change.

WHAT TO DO WITH MOM GUILT

Though we all struggle with feelings of guilt from time to time, mom guilt should not be a mainstay in your life. Never ignore or avoid feelings of guilt. Why? Because if you deal with them, on the other side of that guilt is always freedom. In light of what Christ has done on our behalf, we no longer live under a weight of guilt, condemnation, and shame.

Start by Asking Questions

- What specifically am I feeling guilty about?

- Why do I feel guilty about this? (For example, "None of my friends made this choice," "I heard a Christian Bible teacher say this was wrong," or "It's different from what my own mom did.") The more you can pinpoint the origin of your guilt, the easier it is to identify what type you're dealing with. Don't forget to integrate what you discover about your feelings of guilt with all that you learned in part 3 of this book!

- Is this a vague feeling that's hard to pin down, keeping you trapped in a cycle of fear and condemnation? (For example, "I just feel like a failure as a mom.") Or is this a specific moment in time that has an actionable path toward freedom and repentance? ("I should not have yelled at my children this morning when they couldn't find their shoes.")

For the sake of simplicity, we're going to break down the two main types of mom guilt and how to handle them. Like everything else in this book, we hope you see that this isn't a formula and that there can be a lot of complexities and gray areas as you sort this out.

Type 1: Conviction from the Holy Spirit

Sometimes, we feel guilty because the Holy Spirit is at work in our lives through God's Word and his people to help reveal areas where we are walking in sin. Even though you've repented and believed in Jesus Christ, you're still going to struggle with sin (we all do). Ongoing repentance—turning from your sin and toward God—is an important part of following him.

When we get that sick feeling of conviction in our stomach, or something that we said or did keeps coming to mind and we can't seem to put it at rest, we can examine ourselves and see if we've violated something in God's Word or have failed to love him or others well. If we find that this is the case, we don't have to spend a bunch of time wallowing or beating ourselves up. We can rest in knowing that "if we confess our sins, he is faithful and just and will forgive us our sins and purify us from all unrighteousness."[1]

Note: When God brings conviction, he's not trying to make it as confusing and vague as possible. It's usually clear, tangible, and connected to his Word. He wants us to be able to find freedom!

Action: Pray and confess your sin to the Lord. See where you might need to be restored or make amends with others, and walk forward with God's help, in new choices and habits.

---

[1] 1 John 1:9 NIV.

Type 2: False Guilt

Sometimes we feel guilty because our personal conscience is firing off. We've created an ideal picture of motherhood in our heads as we've gathered images and nice-to-dos from moms we admire or from the words of the culture around us. When we don't live up to those standards or our motherhood looks different from what we planned, it's not that we're in sin; it's that we're disappointed, or sad, or we need to walk in freedom from the expectations of others and ourselves. In this case, we need to shore our hearts up with the truth of God's Word, citing stories, verses, and passages that confirm we're on the right path.

Note: It's the accuser who wants us to be overwhelmed and ineffective as Gospel Moms by making sure we feel as bad and confused as possible. When you are stuck in a mental loop of just feeling terrible at motherhood or feeling like you don't measure up, it's time to stop listening to lies and preach the gospel to yourself.

Action: Pray and ask God to help you remember the truth of what he's done for you in Christ and how he's leading you in your motherhood. Create boundaries around voices or influences that are making you feel like you're not measuring up. Post a verse in your house that will help you speak truth when you're tempted to sink back into guilt.

No matter what path you take—walk forward in freedom from mom guilt!

HELPFUL QUESTIONS FOR DISCERNING RESOURCES

Check Credentials

Who is this person? Are they educated in their field, and if so, where? How are they getting their information, and who else endorses it? What is their reputation? Are they a self-proclaimed expert, or do they have years of firsthand experience, knowledge, and training?

Check Agendas

What type of theology are they hoping their audience adopts? Is there an underlying ideology that influences their ideas? Sometimes you can tell this by seeing who endorses or loves their work.

Check Associations

Who do they "buddy up" with? Are they involved in any questionable or unethical organizations, ministries, or "tribes"? One or two odd associations are probably not concerning, but consider the overall picture of who they spend time with.

Check for the Gospel

What is their worldview? Is it biblical, or is it coming from a different perspective completely? Who or what are they asking you to put your hope and trust in for joy and fulfillment? Is the goal of their message about turning you to Christ or to something else?

Check for False Teaching

Are they sharing the prosperity gospel or a cheap grace mentality? Do they encourage people to hope in something or someone other than Christ (lifestyle, relationship, parenting method, finding the "perfect" balance, and so on)? Do they adhere to cultural relativism, thinking, *Whatever seems good and true to me must be right*?

Testing Resources in Light of the Gospel

Creation: Does this person or resource acknowledge God as the creator and sustainer of all things, as sovereign, and as the one whom we should worship and obey?

Fall: Does this person or resource have the perspective that humans are sinners in need of a Savior? Does it adequately acknowledge the far-reaching impacts of the curse in the brokenness of the world?

Redemption: Does this person or resource encourage you or your children to place your hope in something or someone other than Jesus (a method, a strategy, a lifestyle, and so on)?

Consummation: Does this person or resource point you to the hope of heaven and life after death through belief and trust in Jesus?

Great Commission: Does this person or resource affirm God's main purpose for motherhood—that you are to raise your children in the fear and admonition of the Lord, make disciples, and live with the Bible as the final authority for truth?

Am I in an Echo Chamber?

As you grow in your discernment skills, at times there could be reasons to intentionally seek out resources from other perspectives. Using your own critical thinking skills as you learn from people with different viewpoints, backgrounds, and life experiences, you can discover blind spots that may need to be addressed and develop better reasoning for your own position.

THE ABIDE METHOD

n this book, we've talked a lot about the importance of studying Scripture for yourself to discover God's design for motherhood. At Risen Motherhood, we like to use the Abide Method for studying the Bible. Similar to the inductive Bible study method, it's a way of studying the Bible that puts God first. This isn't the only way to study God's Word, but it's a simple way that doesn't require any special study tools or settings, and we've found it valuable and effective in our own lives. It's called the Abide Method after Jesus's words in John 15 where Jesus exhorts his disciples to "abide in me."[1] *Abide* means to *stay* or *remain*. As believers, we do this in many ways, but a primary one is through intentional study of Scripture. If you're ready to get started with this Bible study method, follow the steps below. Don't worry about doing them all perfectly or feeling like you must complete each step in this order. Use this method to guide your time and provide a general framework, but know that it can be fluid enough to meet the needs of the time you have and the text you are studying. You can do this method on your own or with a group, which is especially helpful for spotting confirmation biases or other areas that require discernment.

---

[1] John 15:4

Before Starting, Gather Your Materials

Scripture: You can write directly in a Bible (like a journaling Bible), or we like to print out the book or passage we're studying on paper in a larger font (10 to 12 point), double-spaced. You can use a search engine to find the Bible passage you'll be studying and copy and paste it into a printable document.

Journal/paper: Grab an empty notebook or loose-leaf paper to jot down notes and thoughts.

Pens/pencils/markers: Some people like to just use one great pen; others use a whole slew of multicolored pencils, pens, or markers.

Begin with Prayer

Before reading and studying the Bible, pray that the Holy Spirit will come and work during your time. Ask that God will open your eyes to new truths, that you will see God as holy as he is, and that God's character, purposes, and plans will come alive as you read.

Build a Framework and Context

When you're first starting to dive into a new book of the Bible, start by reading the book's introduction in a study Bible or a trusted commentary. Read a bit about who the author was, look at any maps or time lines, and research the setting, people, and culture of when and where the text was originally written. Basically, get a feel for the historical and cultural context of the passage. This will help you discover what the text would have sounded like to the original hearers.

Start by answering these questions on an extra sheet of paper or in a notebook:

1. Who wrote it?

2. When was it written?

3. What was the culture and setting like at the time?

4. To whom was it written?

5. Why did they write it?

Once you have some initial framework and context for the book you're about to begin studying, begin with Observation. You'll spend a significant amount of time in this portion of the study, but this is the part that will truly stretch and grow you to understand what the Bible actually says, and it will build the basis for good theology and an understanding of who God is.

Observation: What Does the Text Say?

- Read the text at least once all the way through for comprehension.
- Read again, this time working through the text slowly and deliberately, marking the following:
  key words
  time, locations, and people
  repeated words, ideas, and phrases
  transition words (*but, therefore, because, likewise, if/then*)
  lists (note when the author makes several points in a row)
  contrasts and comparisons
  commands
- As you work through the text, note any questions you have about the meaning of certain words or of the text in general.
- Get out a dictionary. Look up the difficult words you don't know the meaning of. But also look up the keywords in the text (like *holy, sanctification*, and *abide*), even if you think you know what they mean. You'll be surprised by what you discover! Note the appropriate meaning for the passage and any related words.
- Consult different translations for clarity and deeper understanding. (If you don't have hard-copy favorites on hand, we

recommend Bible Gateway. Our go-to translations include the ESV, NIV, CSB, RSV, and NASB.)

- Look up related Scripture (also known as cross-references).

Once you have a clear idea of what the text says, go to Interpretation.

Interpretation: What Does the Text Mean?

- Ask yourself: What would the original hearers have thought?
- Challenge yourself to evaluate how this passage fits within the greater arc of the Bible: Creation, Fall, Redemption, and Consummation.
- Paraphrase: Rewrite the text in your own words.
- Consult reliable commentaries.

After you've discovered the meaning of the text, move to Application.

Application: How Does the Text Change Me?

Answer these questions:

- What does this passage tell you about who God is?
- What does this passage tell you about your sin and need for a Savior? How does it change how you view yourself?
- How can these truths transform your life today?
- Remember that all actions begin as thoughts and desires of the heart. How do these truths transform what you love, worship, and value most?
- In turn, how will these renewed desires change the way you respond to God and others?

- Are there practical things God is leading you to do differently as your heart changes?
- What might these truths look like in action? Is the Holy Spirit bringing to mind any specific people, circumstances, conversations, or sins for your prayer, repentance, and reconciliation?

After you've worked through the Abide Method, here are some ways to respond to what God is teaching you:

- Journal or write down some of these conclusions for further reflection and meditation.
- Share what you learned with a spouse or close friend.
- Pray, repent, and ask God for what you need.

ABOUT THE AUTHORS

Emily A. Jensen and **Laura Wifler** are the cofounders of the Risen Motherhood ministry and cohosts of its chart-topping podcast. They are also in the trenches of motherhood right alongside their readers. With a combination of accessibility, relatability, and solid biblical knowledge, Emily and Laura have a knack for simplifying complex scriptural truths, relating and applying them to everyday life. God has consistently and powerfully used the voices of these two moms to captivate women around the world with the gospel. As sisters-in-law, Emily and Laura both live in central Iowa with their families.

Connect with us:

@emilyajensen and emilyajensen.com

@laurawifler and laurawifler.com

OTHER GOOD READS
FOR GOSPEL MOMS

Discover more from Emily and Laura to help you live out gospel motherhood, grow spiritually strong, and build your child's empathy and imagination.

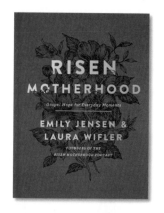

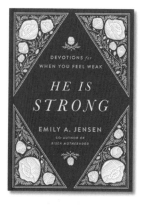
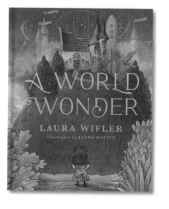
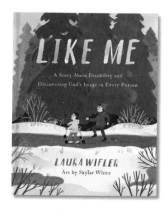